"LORD"
OF THE
DAWN

Quetzalcoatl

and

THE TREE OF LIFE

TONY SHEARER

Naturegraph Publishers

Library of Congress Cataloging-in-Publication Data

Shearer, Tony, 1926 - 2002   Lord of the Dawn
ISBN 0-87961-240-1
Lord of the Dawn illustrated by Tony Shearer

ISBN: 978-0-87961-240-5

Naturegraph Publishers has been publishing books on
natural history, Native Americans, and outdoor subjects
since 1946. Free catalog available

Books for a better world

Naturegraph Publishers, Inc.
PO Box 1047 ● 3543 Indian Creek Rd.
Happy Camp, CA 96039
(530) 493-5353
www.naturegraph.com

DEDICATION

In Memory of Vinson Brown

"He is gone from amongst us.
We will
Miss the sound of his voice,
His face,
We will miss his eyes.
His ears
Will no longer hear the thunder,
The rain
Will no longer fall upon his lips,
His feet
Will no longer leave tracks
In the dirt,
But
He now knows
What we desire to know;
He
Has gone
Beyond the thunder."

......Tony

Publisher's Preface to the 1995 Edition

In this new, revised edition of *Lord of the Dawn*, Tony Shearer has not altered his original story of Quetzalcoatl and the prophecy of Thirteen Heavens and Nine Hells. This remains the same as before. But certain minor sections of the first edition, which deviated from the main theme and contained information mostly found in scholarly books, have been removed. As a result, the story is now imbued with a new clarity and freshness, while faithfully preserving the message of Tony's version of the Quetzalcoatl myth.

The author has also written a prelude to the feature story in which he tells his readers how he learned the story while visiting the Valley of Oaxaca in Mexico, how *Lord of the Dawn* first came to be published, what transpired in the succeeding twenty-three years since its publication, and how the prophecy has been fulfilled.

The book concludes with a new afterword by the author and some useful background history on the sacred calendar, the Eagle Bowl, the little people, and the great tree at Oaxaca.

Tony Shearer is well qualified to write on the subject of ancient Mexico. Besides writing *Lord of the Dawn*, he is also author of *Beneath the Moon and Under the Sun: A Poetic Reappraisal of the Sacred Calendar and the Prophecies of Ancient Mexico*, *The Praying Flute: Song of the Earth Mother*, and *Children of the Sun: How Music Came to Earth*.

Acknowledgements

This second edition of *Lord of the Dawn* could not have been accomplished without the encouragement and assistance of my publishers. And so it is with particular thanks to Barbara Brown, and with the fondest memories of her husband, my friend Vinson, who unfortunately will never see this edition of a book he loved, that the story continues. But I believe that Vinson's prayers go with us, prayers for the future of the living, and prayers for the yet unborn. I am grateful to Dennis DeSart for his work on the editing end of things.

When I set out to deliver this revised version of *Lord of the Dawn* in the summer of 1990, I believed that my readers were entitled to a conclusion regarding the prophecy that has made this work so unique. In my enthusiasm to present a suitable answer, I all but destroyed the innocence of the work, creating a terrible likeness to the original story. For two years I battered my head against a brick wall. So all consuming was the project that, in the midst of this dilemma, my health gave out, and I was forced to visit a doctor. After several tests the announcement came—prostate cancer was degenerating my pelvis bone, six little tumors were found on my skull, and spots ran down my spine. I had suddenly become a victim of prostate cancer. I felt alone, abandoned, and helpless. Not only this, but a burning desire to finish this work agitated my soul. I feared I might not be able to complete the task or to fulfill my debt to a certain Zapotec woman named Alicia who had introduced me to the seers and wise ones among her people, and who shared my love of this story. Then, out of the blue, Kathy Kent, a lady I scarcely knew, found me, bringing a light into my darkness. Through her integrity as a woman and a healer, she hacked away the negativity I had soaked myself in. I cleaned up my diet, started to curb my ego, and rediscovered my own higher power.

After that I found a physician, a true healer, and of all things, a traditional flute player. But more than all else, a friend. His name is H. Louden Kiracoft, who is now retired in the haunts of nature. Through Louden I learned the way to my healing and met the kind and thoughtful people at Tap Pharmaceuticals, the distributors of Lupron depot 7.5 mg., which helped save my life. I recommend Lupron to every man who faces this illness. Prostate cancer is not necessarily the end of the world. For me it has become a new beginning, a beginning that also came through the grace of two remarkable women who helped me to clear my mind of fears and self doubt. They are Patsy Crandall and Karen Mischke. I thank you both.

My cancer is now in remission, and my life has come back to me. I thank all of you who helped me on the way, friends, family, mountain spirits, canyon spirits, Black Raven, the great tree, and the Zapotec woman I met there. Above all else, thank you God!

The picture I painted for the cover of this edition is purely the world of the little people. I call it "The Place of Many Rainbows." The river is the River Tawasentha, the canyon it flows from is "Moon Flower," the big old tree you see in the distance is "Many Trees." It represents the special trees we humans hold in our hearts. I call the mountain range you see there the "Altim Elut Mountains" (spelled backwards—Mitla Tule Mountains). Altim Elut is a pockwatchie chief who plays a major role in many of my stories about the little people. In the foreground you see me praying up the sun with my old Lakota flute. I'm sitting there like a pockwatchie, among the fallen logs and leaves where mushrooms grow. And if you look closely you'll see a pockwatchie sitting there too. That's Quill. He is an old friend of mine. He was the one who inspired the painting. The knot hole in the fallen tree is my pathway, when I'm ready, back into the earth again. Death is a loving mother, calling her children home. In the sky you see the Morning Star—who else but my adopted Dad, old Quetzalcoatl—shining bright. The sun, dawning in royal red, is the Glory of God. The temple in the distance is not a ruin. Far from it, that temple is the only temple that escaped the wrath of the conquerors. It is the "Golden Temple of Quetzalcoatl," which you will find enshrined in the hearts of millions of Indian people who never gave up the dream. In the sky, if you look closely, you will see two birds flying into the dawn. That's Alicia and I, in our aspect of two black ravens, finally winging home to Oaxaca. I have named the painting "Pockwatchie Muse, Spirit of the Dawn."

PRELUDE

The Quest and Manuscript: A New 'Flight of Quetzalcoatl'

It was 1970 when a weathered, tired, and hungry man showed up on the door step of Naturegraph Publishers in Healdsburg, California. He carried a bundle under his arm. The bundle contained a manuscript. He said that he had traveled far, all the way from the banks of the Rio Grande River in New Mexico. He said that he hoped Vinson and Barbara Brown, owners of Naturegraph, would read the manuscript, and judge whether it was worthy of printing. The couple invited the stranger in and asked if he would spend the night, and join the family for the evening meal.

After dinner the stranger told them his story. In many ways it was a sad story...how he had lost his wife and children, resigned from his job with Time Life Broadcasting and CBS Television. How he had become a revolutionist, and an activist for Indian and Chicano rights. His story was filled with fire and anger as he told of the atrocities he had seen committed against Indian people in Mexico and Central America. Then he showed them his five-hole Lakota flute. He explained how the flute was his voice to God, his voice to the Great Mystery, how he had "prayed" it across America, over all the dying rivers.

After many stories of adventure, he began to speak about Oaxaca, Mexico. As he did, it became apparent that Oaxaca was very important to him. Tears formed in his eyes when he spoke of the beautiful Zapotec Indians he had shared so much of his life with. How he longed to return and live those days once more. He told of how he met his muse, his lady of inspiration, Alicia, from whom he learned many, many things. On mountain trails and on city streets they had explored each other's worlds together, and she had brought him to meet many of the old men and old women who had kept alive the ancient stories, as they passed down from generation to generation. He learned to count from the old men, keepers of the calendar, and he learned something of the meaning of the numbers. He recalled the ancient temples of Monte Alban, Mitla, Zaachila and Yalalag. He said that in the Valley of Oaxaca, in the village of Santa Maria del Tule, he had found the Tree of Life. "It's the biggest tree in all the world," he said. "My manuscript tells about the tree, about Quetzalcoatl, and about their relationship to each other."

He had visited the ancient ruins again and again, ate tamales, papaya, móle, corn tortillas with the people. He learned the way they offer their prayers to God. He camped on mountain trails with shepherds, explored crazy caverns, tramped the trails of ancient demi-gods, and slept in the arms of the tree. Learning from crones and wizards, he had sought all that they would teach him. The haunted tombs of heroes, the temples of magicians, the forgotten hidden language, he studied every word, as well as mathematics, calendars, hieroglyphics, incantations from the stars. He mapped the ancient ruins, measured pyramids and temples, and learned the rites of passage from the priesthood of the dead.

He pointed to his manuscript, and said, "I have named my book LORD OF THE DAWN. It's about how he walked upon the earth. It tells of how he was born as a man, gave honor to his sacred mother, praised his warrior father, and paid homage to the great tree. It is about his life on earth, how he lived, toiled, and suffered so the races of man would prosper. He brought peace to the earth."

The stranger went on with the story about his manuscript. He said that he had written it under less than favorable conditions. He had secured a primitive home in the village of the great tree. In that village he had started the story. It was a struggle from the beginning. He had no tools except pencil and paper, so the first draft was written by hand. As he wrote he collected ideas, stories and feelings. But he ran out of money and returned to New Mexico, where he completed the work in a tent on the banks of the Rio Grande, not far from Los Alamos. His story was filled with the frustrations of being poor. "One day my boss was CBS Television," he explained, "then the next day I was a half-breed Indian, living in a tent, making my living selling Aztec calendars that I cast in plaster. It was a crazy existence—hunger, cold, lack of the most common comforts. But I wrote the book. I wrote my book about Quetzalcoatl."

Then he told of how he had met a group of Bahá'ís, and how they seemed to understand his message. He said, "one of them was a kind lady, who helped me by putting the work into finished form. She made grammatical corrections, and typed the words for me on her typewriter. She helped me get the job done." At last he laid the manuscript down and said, "in this work there is a prophecy that has never been told before. It is not a vague prophecy, in fact, it gives the exact date that it will happen...and I know that one day this prophecy will shake the world." Then with one hand on his manuscript, he brought his flute clearly into sight, and said, "The prophecy given here declares that on August 16, 1987, a new world will be born, and from that new world, a new race will walk upon the earth. I truly believe that it will happen. That is why I say that it is an earth shaking prophecy."

Needless to say, the weathered stranger was me. When I look back at it now, I have to laugh at my own drama, my partnership in the human comedy, how I felt driven to save the world from...the world. Dear Vinson Brown, a great naturalist and author in his own right, was absolutely fascinated with my use of the little people, the earth spirits, *pockwatchies* and *tlaloques*. No one has ever used these little spirits in this way before. Little people, only two inches tall, guardians of the Earth Mother, servants of the Lord of the Dawn. In 1971, "earth spirits" needed some explanation. Now, in 1995, they seem to be in the hearts of all of us. The human race has taken up its job. Many people have learned that rivers can actually die, mountains can really be murdered. But it is not polluted cities that create polluted people, it is the other way around. In my manuscript these little earth guardians came from the clouds when the clouds (a male force) fell in love with the earth (a female force). Needless to say, in poetic myth, such things as that can happen. The cloud had given his all to her. He had created rivers and washed mountains—he was crazy about his lovely lady, the earth.

"This is a love story," I told the Browns. Its history lies deep in the heart of ancient America. The story is set within the framework of a terrible yet wonderful prophecy: the prophecy of the thirteen heavens and the nine hells. The prophecy was carved on the rocks of the sacred city of Palenque in southern Mexico more than fifteen hundred years ago. Carved in glyphs and based on intricate mathematical calculations, it called for the near to utter destruction of all things in Indian America, but it promised a beautiful and harmonious new world for those who keep the covenant with the Creator and the earth mother. Thus:

> *"All things that must be*
> *must be in balance, and*
> *that takes practice."*

"A love story?" asked Vinson. "What about your Quetzalcoatl, is he part of your love story?"

"Yes," I said. "In a certain way he is the heart and the soul of the love story. He and the sacred tree really make up the story." Quetzalcoatl and the great tree are the reason that I wrote the story down in the first place. You see, the tree is the symbol of all of nature, the Tree of Life. And Quetzalcoatl, because of what he is to the earth, and to all Indian people, is the voice of every manifestation of God since the beginning of time. He is speaking to all of us about our mother the earth. I began to understand when I fell in love with Alicia, my lady of inspiration. She taught me of the love between the earth mother and the Lord of the Dawn, a love that gave birth to the great tree.

The name Quetzalcoatl (ket-sal-ko-atl) comes from the Nahuatl language of central Mexico, but he is much older even than that language. His origin is believed to have been on the coast of Mexico, where he was identified with the sea and the wind. He has always been worshiped as a creator god. His history and his myth are forever intertwined, like the plumed serpent, which is a graphic and literal representation of his name, Quetzalcoatl. He is also the Sacred Twin, God of Wind and Air, Breath of Life. He was identified with the morning star, and thus called the Lord of the Dawn. As an evolving god, his myth and history can be traced through the evolution of all of Mexico, a history which is easily three thousand years old.

In 947 AD, it is believed, he was born as a man. His mother, Chimalma, was a temple virgin. She was supposedly a reincarnation of the goddess of love and flowers. His father was the old warrior, Mixcoatl (mish-ko-atl), the famous leader of a fierce tribe of nomads from the northern deserts, called the Chichimeca. Their son, Ce Acatl, in turn, was the incarnation of the ancient creator god, Quetzalcoatl, who was destined to become the most famous culture hero of ancient Mexico. He was a divine sage, priest, and ruler, responsible for revealing many arts and sciences to the mighty Toltec people. His teachings were so Christ-like that the Catholic authorities at the time of the conquest (1519-1521) believed him to be Saint Thomas the Apostle, and they continued to believe that for the next three hundred years. *LORD OF THE DAWN*, is about all of this.

My manuscript became a book, and as I had promised, I took it to the world. For me, the combination of my flute and the book, and the memory of my lady of inspiration, constituted a new 'Flight of Quetzalcoatl'. To that end I dedicated my life, using theater as my vehicle, the stage as my pulpit, and the prophecy as my theme. I blitzed the planet with my message. To be sure, I was not alone. The Southern Ute Tribe, El Teatro Campesino, International Theatre Institute, the National Theatre of Poland, the Irish Ballet, the Blind Theatre of Paris, the Iowa Theater Lab, even some people in the State Department, and many more people helped.

Theatre became my home. I learned the art of living out of a suitcase and became a rootless vagabond, a master of guerrilla theater, a trickster and a flute player on stage, a mad knight on a tightrope. These were one night stands mostly, restaurant food, cheap hotels, and fleeting relationships. My theater was of my own making. It was as colorful as a gypsy circus, militant as a Black Panther at a KKK meeting, and as enduring as a T-bone steak at a vegetarian banquet. But my book was always held in a place of honor, and has been respected by many people.

I traveled the world over, played my flute, told the prophecy, made television shows, and chalked up a resume that looked like an index to a book about Sinbad the Sailor. I came to know the true meaning of the words, "the earth is my mother." After a while it mattered little to me whether I was in Africa with the Zulu or in India with Mother Theresa—people are the same everywhere. I learned to love people for what they are, and for what they are not. We people of the world are truly only one people, one world with one hope—to live and let live. We will have to give up greed and cruelty, have more compassion, live lives of loyalty, and accept each other as brothers and sisters.

As the years passed, age crept in and time grew short. I slowed down and the world was changing too fast around me. Fears of failing began to grip my heart. What if August 16, 1987 comes and nothing happens? What if August 16 comes and everything happens? What if the whole world mistakes me for a prophet? Think of what the world does to prophets! And the greatest fear of all, "What about all the people who trusted me and believed in the new world I sang of...what about them? The fear was real, and by 1984 this fear was crashing into my dreams every night. "For every action there is an equal and opposite reaction." I was exhausted and worn out, and I was doubting my vision. Had my life been a waste of time? Had all of this been only an illusion that was now becoming a nightmare? The day of the prophecy was at hand, and I had become a frightened and tired old man. An old man with an impossible dream.

August 16, 1987 came and went. The prophecy was true—for those with the eyes to see it. Millions of people all over the world rose up and honored it. But even millions more had never heard of it. For some, it was a day of exploitation; a good day to make a buck. But for most it was a day of reverence, and the New Age had been born. Perhaps the Bahá'ís understood it more clearly than anyone, because, independently, they promised the "Lesser Peace." August 16, 1987 lives on in our hearts. Never give up the dream, the hope! Fight on in peace. Someday we will win. The world cannot long endure under non-spiritual ways of thinking.

The valley of Oaxaca was as jammed as a worn out Indian bus that day. People came from all over the world to behold the great tree, and maybe to find Quetzalcoatl there. The prophecy shook the world...but not enough to awaken us completely. Not enough to mend the lives broken by greed and cruelty, not enough to unite the planet under one banner dedicated to freedom and justice for all. But there are millions of people who truly believe that a *new world* should happen, that some day in the future, when we finally get it right, it will happen. Maybe, it already has. All we can do now is wait and see.

I am a storyteller of poetic myth. I think of myself as a myth maker, and this book has been my most successful story, although you can see it has cost me much. It has afforded me both fame and sorrow, blessed me and cursed me. The book has been burned by some religious sects. It has been a source of inspiration for many young and eager Native American and Chicano poets and artists. It inspired Tony Vann to create his rock opera, *Lord of the Dawn*. It has been called blasphemy and it has been called classic. A famous scholar called it the greatest hoax since *The Book of Mormon*. Another author drew from this and other works of mine to create works of "his own." The history of this book has reached legendary proportions. I am proud of this work for many reasons. Foremost among these is that it has endured in the marketplace for twenty-three years. More than all else, I am thankful that my muse and I were instrumental in awakening the process of the Plumed Serpent—old Quetzalcoatl.

I am often asked by students: "If Quetzalcoatl was alive today how would we know him?" My answer to that question is always the same. "Quetzalcoatl is as alive today as he has even been. You will find him in your heart. He is the voice that teaches you to be loyal and compassionate to your friends and loved ones. He is the echo that tells you the earth is truly your Mother, that the sky is truly your Father. His is the teaching that tells us again and again that respect for the rights of others is peace, that we should make every act in our life a creative one, create beauty, inspire peace and harmony, create trust, aid the weak and needy, and pray and meditate daily. Above all else be honest to your own heart." Quetzalcoatl lives, as always, in the good things of the world, the same place that Christ, Buddha, Mohammed, and Bahá'u'lláh will be found, healing the pains of us all.

LORD

OF THE

DAWN

Quetzalcoatl

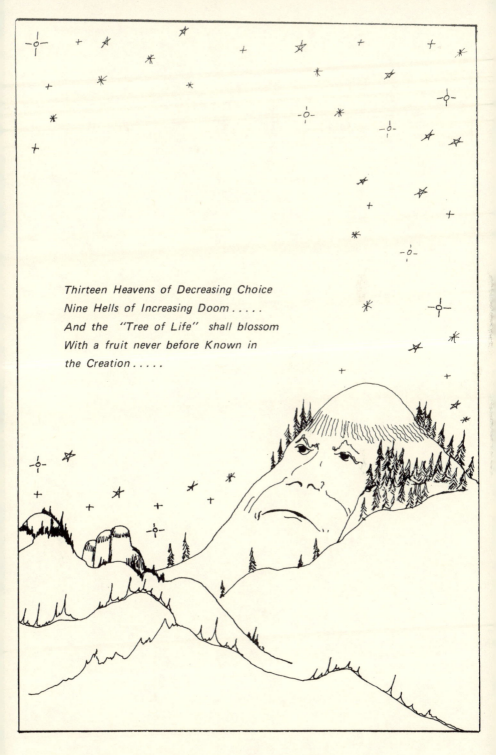

Thirteen Heavens of Decreasing Choice
Nine Hells of Increasing Doom . . . . .
And the "Tree of Life" shall blossom
With a fruit never before Known in
the Creation . . . . .

OUT OF THE MIST

The Universe.
The Planet.
And
Somewhere
In all of this---
The earth---
And
Man!
And now
Man's
Quest to explore it,
And
To make that
His tomorrow

Yet,
Since the dawn of logic
Man has posed the haunting questions:
"Who are we?"
And,
"From where did we come?"
The remains of ancient man
Literally
Cover the surface
Of the earth.
But where are the
Oldest Remains?

And
There
Are those who ask:
"DID we come from the earth,
Or
Did we come from another galaxy?
A world
Beyond the limits
Of our imagination!

Did
We come from the legendary Atlantis?
Or,
Was that story
Only a myth?"
"Did
The same Master Builders
Of the pyramids of Egypt
Also
Build the Pyramid of the Sun
In Mexico?"

"Who was
The white bearded man
Who came to Mexico
And taught
The strange philosophy
Of Peace?"

-o-

Was He a Toltec Lord
Or,
Was He
The last survivor
From
A civilization
Which rests on the floor
Of the Pacific?
How
Can we
Learn the answers
To
These questions?

How
Do we
Know what is true
And
What is only imagination?

We ask the people who have made
A life study of man,
Of man's ancient history.
We ask an archeologist.
And
If the archeologist really knows
He points
To the remains
Of ancient man
And
His answer is swift.

Man evolved on this planet.
The oldest remains of man
Are no doubt in Africa.
Atlantis is a myth.

There is no connection
Between
The civilizations of
Mexico
And
Egypt.

The Bearded God of Mexico
Was not a white man.
He was a Mexican.
A Mexican-Indian.
A Toltec.

And. . . .
There are no remains
on the floor of the Pacific.

How does the archeologist know this:

      Because

      It is his business

      To scientifically

      Dig into the earth

      And

      Bring forth

      The remains of ancient man

      And

      To assemble those remains

      Into an honest history

      Of that civilization.

      But, as certain as

      The archeologists are,

      They are the first to admit

      They do not know it all,

      And

      On some parts of the earth

      They may be very wrong, or

      Know almost nothing at all.

MUSEUM

THE PEOPLE OF THE CLOUDS

The valley of Oaxaca is
> The homeland
> Of the Zapotecs,
> The People of the Clouds.

The climate in Oaxaca is
> Fair the year around.
> The elevation
> About five thousand two hundred feet
> Above the sea.

In all the world
> I doubt
> There are people
> More gentle
> Than the Zapotecs,
> Nor
> People
> Who have been more abused
> By outside forces.

They have been discriminated against
In their own land,
Hated,
And at times
Feared..

Yet,
Isn't this
The story
Of all Indian peoples?

But,
The Zapotec emerges
Victorious
As Indians will be victorious.

They
Insist on
Being understood.

And that understanding begins
At the summit
Of their Sacred Mountain,
In the ancient ruins of Monte Alban.
In the ancient temples
Of the Zapotec.

A map
Shows the excavated
Area of Monte Alban.
But
One must remember
That the entire city
Once
Covered a
Twenty-five square mile area,

Mostly
On the mountain top,
The ridges,
And
Natural points;

Temples,
Observatories,
Astronomical shrines
And
Sacred Altars,
Pyramids,
Sunken courts,
And stairways.

The tomb area is
To the north,
Beyond the giant stairway.

All of this
is only a fraction
Of the ancient city.

What mysteries lie
Buried
Under those mounds?

What strange people
Transformed
A living stone
Into a temple?

Temples
To
Forgotten Gods.

It is said the ghosts
        Of the ancients
        Still
        Visit these ruins.

        Here
        The old God,
        Quetzalcoatl,
        Still fights human suffering.

        The Rain God
        Still brings the rain
        And
        The Corn God
        Still brings the crops.

        To understand,
        We must know
        Something
        Of the logic
        Of all Mexican Indians,

        Perhaps
        The root
        Logic
        Of all mankind.

THE ROOTS OF THE SACRED TREE

The Indians of Mexico
  Worshipped
  The physical forces
  Of nature.

  They
  Built temples
  To their Gods,
  Found magic
  In the clouds.

When
There was no water,
When
The rains failed to fall
From the sky,
They
Would call upon
The sky serpent
Call upon their Gods,
the Servants
of the Great Spirit.
For clouds,
For rain.

There was magic in that cool rain,
It turned the corn green
And
Filled the rivers.

They found magic in the lightning
and the thunder ---
The voice
And the hand
Of The Lord of Creation.

They were amazed
By the force
Of the ocean,
Amazed
By its mighty sound!

Good things came from the ocean,
Food,
And
Mystery.

It was good.

Jungles held dark mysteries,
    Secrets.

Wild flowers grew there
    And
    The Indians named them,
    The star flowers,
    Fire flowers
    The lightning flowers
    Flowers of the rains.

The jungle was the home of
    Bright colored parrots
    And
    Chattering monkeys.

    It
    Was the home
    Of night animals,
    Big cats.

The Jaguar was a God
    In disguise!
    He
    Was endowed with
    Supernatural powers.

    The Jaguar
    Had once
    Destroyed
    The earth,
    Devoured mankind.

The jungle was
    Full of wonder,
    And
    Magic.

But, the heavenly bodies,
   The stars,
   were the greatest mysteries.
   The rotation,
   Their disappearing
   And
   Reappearing
   Gave wonder
   To the mind.

The Indians measured
   Time
   And space
   religiously.

   They
   calculated
   An absolutely
   accurate calendar.

   This was only accomplished
   By
   Constant observation
   Of the stars.

   Every day
   The sun
   Must fight
   The stars
   From the sky.

   Every night
   He
   must die.

   The sun
   Was a warrior
   And
   Held great power
   As a God.

Yagul polychrome

Pot sherd from Oaxaca

Mitla polychrome

Fragment of serpent head

Everything in nature
>Had
>To be balanced
>In religion.
>The serpent
>Was balanced,
>So were the
>Brightly feathered birds.

>Thus
>Came the feathered serpent!
>He
>Was also
>The planet Venus
>And
>The West Wind.

So it was with everything,
>A constant fight
>Of
>Good against evil,
>Light against dark.
>Until
>At last
>They had formed
>A vast and fantastic civilization.

>"Could this be heaven?"
>Asked
>An early Spaniard
>When
>First he saw
>Tenochtitlan
>Now Mexico City.

>Unbelievable!
>Fantastic!

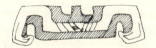

A
Vast civilization
Of barbaric splendor,
Pagan worship in its
Most magnificent form,
Vision seekers.

Yes, it was these things
And more.
More fantastic than we can imagine
More incredible than you would
Ever dream.

When archeologists first saw Monte Alban,
It was only
High earth mounds,
Very unimpressive.

Some scientists feel
It would have been cheaper
To build a city
Of this size
Than
To excavate one.

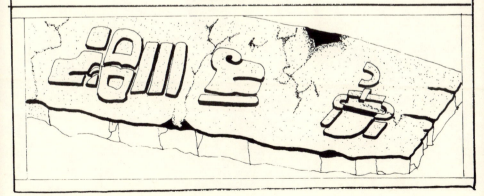

IN THE BEGINNING

The Earth was a virgin,
        nothing grew from her.
        No trees
        Nor flowers,
        No mountains
        And no streams.
She was only
        endless matter,
        turning through
        endless space.

She was lonely
        and tired
        of waiting
        for something to create.

Then the Clouds
        found the Earth
        and the Earth
        felt the
        Clouds surround her
        and she felt the
        thrill of
        Life in her spirit.

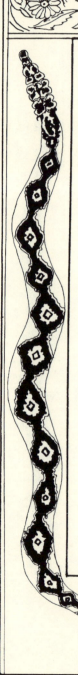

She
was no longer
alone.
Now,
She could create.
And the Clouds
Found the Earth to be
What the Clouds
Had always wanted,
A place to stop
And
A place to create.

Then the Clouds
gathered together in
Great excitement.
The Clouds
grew dark
With the weight of Creativeness,
With the weight of love.

And the Clouds
rained down
upon the Earth.

And she,
The Earth,

Reached up
To touch the Clouds
With mountains of stone
From her breast.

And the

Creative forces of the Clouds
Washed the mountains
And
Formed the rivers.

Then, she,

The Earth
Released the seeds
Of her flesh
And
Trees sprang forth
with leaves.

And grass

Leaped from her flesh
To meet
The fresh rain.
Bushes,
And reeds,
And flowers
Sprang into being,
As a result of
Her love for the rain.

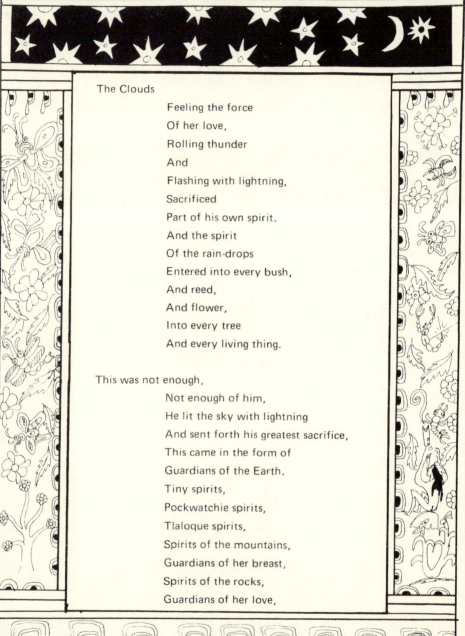

The Clouds

> Feeling the force
> Of her love,
> Rolling thunder
> And
> Flashing with lightning,
> Sacrificed
> Part of his own spirit.
> And the spirit
> Of the rain-drops
> Entered into every bush,
> And reed,
> And flower,
> Into every tree
> And every living thing.

This was not enough,

> Not enough of him,
> He lit the sky with lightning
> And sent forth his greatest sacrifice,
> This came in the form of
> Guardians of the Earth.
> Tiny spirits,
> Pockwatchie spirits,
> Tlaloque spirits,
> Spirits of the mountains,
> Guardians of her breast,
> Spirits of the rocks,
> Guardians of her love,

Spirits of the Rivers
Guardians of her blood,
Spirits of the valleys,
Guardians of her growth,
Spirits
For all things
of the Earth,
And
No particle of dust
Nor grain of sand
Was left
Without
Part of his spirit.

And the "Little People" danced
    Through the darkness
    On the Earth,
    Singing
    The love song
    The Clouds
    Had taught them.

And the Earth,
    now radiant
    with their creation,
    Brought forth her own water.
    It came in the form of tears,
    Tears of love

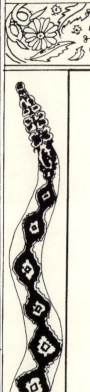

And
Tears of joy.
And
Those tears
Are called springs.

Then the Creator of the Clouds and the Earth
Saw what had happened
When His creations had met
And He said,
"It is not yet finished,
Now I will give form."

Deer were first,
Serpents next,
Eagles and wolves followed,
Hawks and dogs came
Birds with bright feathers
And all the insects
And all of the reptiles
And animals came,
And
All things that live
Have their own story
And
Their own reason
For being.

Then the Creator examined it all
        And said,

        "GOOD.

        Now I will make humans,"
        And immediately
        A man
        Sprang from the oldest Tree on Earth,
And in that same instant
        A woman sprang from the same Tree.
        And that Tree is the "Tree of Life."
When they reached
        The dirt,
        And stood up,
        They started
        To look for
        Each other in the darkness.
When they found each other
        They started to look for food.
They looked for a long time,
        Walked many miles in the darkness,
        Crossed many rivers
        And
        Drank the tears
        Of many Springs.

When at last

        they found themselves

        back at the "Tree of Life"

        They said,

        "Tree, we are hungry,

        Where is food?"

And the "Tree of Life" said,

        "Take a leaf from me,

        And

        Put it in your Earth Mother

        And

        You shall have the perfect food."

The man and the woman took a leaf

        From the ancient Tree

        And

        Put it in the flesh of their

        Earth Mother

        And

        A stalk of corn appeared.

And at that same moment

        The woman had two babies (twins)

And at that same moment

        The sun was born.

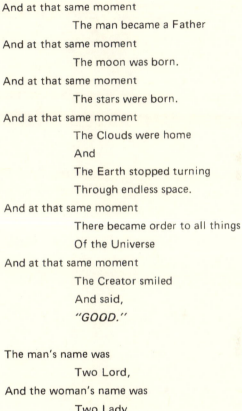

And at that same moment
    The man became a Father
And at that same moment
    The moon was born.
And at that same moment
    The stars were born.
And at that same moment
    The Clouds were home
    And
    The Earth stopped turning
    Through endless space.
And at that same moment
    There became order to all things
    Of the Universe
And at that same moment
    The Creator smiled
    And said,
    "GOOD."

The man's name was
    Two Lord,
And the woman's name was
    Two Lady
    And they had two sons,
    And they lived in the
    "Land of Two."

They went to Monte Alban
       And built a Temple
       And an observatory
       And made altars
       And shrines
       And Holy Places to
       Bury their dead.

Here on Monte Alban they learned
       The mysteries of the stars,
       Measured time
       And studied the Spirits
       of the earth.
They came to know
       And to love
       Every raindrop,
       Because they knew,
       "The same Power
       that created That spirit
       Had created them."
       And
       They are the People,
       They are the Zapotec.

The Zapotec
       came to know

The Creator of all things,
came to know
And
To love the Rain,
The Clouds,
And
came to know
And love
The tears of the Earth Mother.
They often went to visit
The "Tree of Life."
And sometimes
The Tree would
remind them:

"Look around
see the Earth
Look at the sky
Count the Stars
Feel the Sun
Taste the rain
Touch your Brother
Know your Sister
Love each other.

Breathe the Air
Taste the water
And eat your food--
But remember---
It is a gift
All of this------
Is a gift
Know it well. . . . .

You are here to learn
you will be tested. . . .

Learn the science of the Creation
Teach the science 'Love of the
Creator'. . . . . . ."

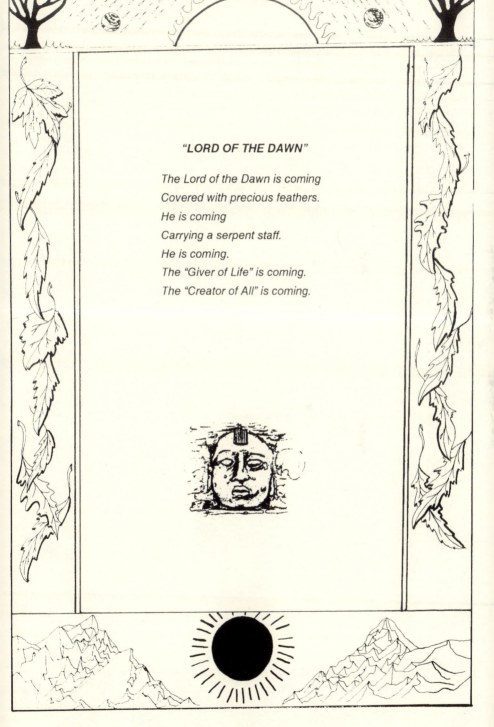

"LORD OF THE DAWN"

The Lord of the Dawn is coming
Covered with precious feathers.
He is coming
Carrying a serpent staff.
He is coming.
The "Giver of Life" is coming.
The "Creator of All" is coming.

The old magician,
>> the sorcerer of Monte Alban
>> Studied
>> The Charts of Time,
>> Read
>> The old prophecies.

Then
>> He stood up
>> And
>> Untied his robe,
>> Letting it fall in a heap
>> At his feet.
>> He turned to the altar
>> Of Cosijo (the rain god)
>> And
>> With many gestures
>> Of his hands
>> And
>> His body
>> He prayed
>> In this way:

"Two heavens of time have we waited.
Now
The cycle of the second heaven is near its close.
Now
The time has come for your return.

"Let it be true:
Let it not be the imagining of foolish people,
Of wistful people.
Let it be true.

"Two heavens of time have we waited.
Let it be now."

The prophecies of the Manifestation were well-known to the
people of Ancient Mexico.

And when the time grew near
>   The people
>   Felt the fulfillment
>   More in their hearts
>   Than
>   In their logic.

The news of the nearness of the
>   "Promised Day"
>   Spread throughout the land.
>   From seashore to seashore
>   The word
>   Was carried.
>   "He is coming."

In the Maya Land,
>   From Guatemala
>   To Yucatan
>   The people listened,
>   And listened,
>   And looked around.
>   They studied
>   What
>   They could see.
>   And what they saw
>   Was bad.

The Maya, who had hosted the Lord of the Dawn
>   In the beginning,
>   Had,
>   Since his departure,
>   Turned away from him
>   And
>   Taken up the earthly pleasures
>   Of
>   The Jaguar Cult.

Now,

> The people studied
> What they had done.
> "We have been wrong!"
> They said at last,
> *"We*
> *didn't believe*
> *It could be.*

But now

> *We feel it in our hearts,*
> *See the changes in our children.*

Now

> *We must right the wrong."*

The Jaguar Clans were murdered,

> Their temples burned,
> Their idols smashed.

The entire Mayan civilization crumbled

> Into pathetic ruins.
> And the people
> Rushed
> From the burning cities
> To the forest
> And attempted
> To build new temples
> To
> The Lord of the Dawn.
> Build a temple in His honor,
> Build a temple to the Morning Star,
> Build a shrine to the Tree of Life,
> *"Hurry*
> *He is coming. . . ."*

The Valley of Oaxaca was no exception.

> The magical powers
> Of the Jaguar Cult
> Had long held the people in thrall,
> But
> With the word of His coming

The Zapotec rose up
In religious rebellion
And
Crushed the source
That
Had enslaved their minds.

So it was throughout the land.
Indication of this prophecy's
fulfillment
Has been found
In such distant places as
Saint Louis, Missouri,
The Ohio River mounds,
In the Rio Grande Valley
And as far South as
Columbia
And Peru,
An area roughly,
nine times as large as the
Holy Land
And as large
As the civilized part of
Ancient China.

The ruins of Tikal
In Guatemala, that
Had
An estimated population of 100,000
people,
was abandoned
And
Was left in ruins
At this time.
Tikal
was the home
of the greatest
of the Jaguar Clans.

Monte Alban, some twenty-five square miles
　　　　　of religious barracks,
　　　　　temples,
　　　　　Pyramids
　　　　　And
　　　　　Astronomical structures,
　　　　　Was abandoned
　　　　　By the Zapotec.

　　　　　(Later,
　　　　　It thrived again
　　　　　Under Mixtec lords.)

　　　　　City after city
　　　　　Was abandoned
　　　　　And
　　　　　Left in ruin,
　　　　　Old religious cults
　　　　　Were destroyed.

But high in the Sierras,
　　　　　South of present day Mexico City,
　　　　　Stood the old temples of Quetzalcoatl
　　　　　At a place called Xochicalco.

There
　　　　　The order of Quetzalcoatl,
　　　　　Had retreated
　　　　　After the fall of Teotihucan
　　　　　One hundred and four years before.
　　　　　And the old Priests
　　　　　Of Quetzalcoatl
　　　　　Held
　　　　　The prophecy in order.

　　　　　They knew
　　　　　What no one else knew.

For
They had been chosen
As the Guardians of His sacred Tablets.
They knew
When he would be born,
They knew
He would be born there,
At Xochicalco.

They waited
And waited,
But
The day had not yet come
And
They knew it.

"Thirteen Heavens of Decreasing Choice, Nine
Hells of Increasing Doom----

Thirteen, 52-year cycles of Choice; Nine, 52-year
cycles of Doom

"And the "Tree of Life" shall blossom
With a fruit never before known in the creation.
And that fruit shall be the New Spirit of Men."

Where had this come from?
The Priests of Xochicalco knew.
They knew it had come from the source.
They knew it came
From the City of the Serpent,
From the jungle low-lands,
long ago,
When He appeared on Earth.
They knew
He had left this prophecy behind
and
Told them

He would return to remind them
And
To enlighten them.

"You will not know me by my miracles," He had said.
"Magicians can perform miracles.
You will know me by the 'Tree',
But
We *will* do miracles," He said.

His signs were many,
The Morning Star,
The Sacred Twin,
The Tree of Life,
The Feathered Serpent,
But now,

The Lord of the Dawn is coming!

THE MOTHER OF THE DAWN

"Come quickly",
  Cried the children.
  "We found her in the bushes,
  She is alone
  And
  She is hurt,
  Covered with mud,
  And
  Scratched by thorn bushes
  She has walked far
  And
  She has come to see
  Her uncle Salavi,
  She is hurt,
  She is pretty."

Chimalma had arrived,
  Niece of Old Salavi,
  The elder of Xochicalco.

She was taken to a bed
  And made comfortable
  Washed
  And fed
  And covered with a
  Soft cotton blanket
  And
  She slept
  For a day
  And a night.

When she woke
  Salavi was beside her
  And she wept.

Salavi comforted her
And asked
Of her father, his brother,
Dead,
She said.

He asked of her mother, his friend,
Her answer
Was the same.
Dead.

Then she told him what had happened.
Told him of her love,
Told him of the barbarians
And he said
He knew that, and that now
He knew her part in this long story.

He asked
If she would come to the temple,
And tell the Council of Quetzalcoatl
Her story.
She said that
She would do that.

So Salavi went to the "Shrine of the Dawn"
and prayed
Until he was told that she was
At the temple of
The Council of Quetzalcoatl
Then
He went there to hear her,
And
To help.

"I was washing my hair in a waterfall
And he came then
And watched me.

At first
I was afraid,
But
He was not as bad as he looked.
He was a warrior
Of the Chichimeca:
He was their leader.
His name,
Mixcoatl, (Cloud Serpent),
He followed me home
And
Talked to my father.

Mixcoatl wanted me,
Wanted me to be his wife,
He wanted me to
Make children for him.
He said he would make a good world
For everyone,
So our children could live in beauty.

No, said my father,
My father told him that I was
Chimalma
A virgin of the Temple of the Dawn,
I could not marry.

Mixcoatl was not young,
He was an older man,
His love for me
Was strong and pure,
I could realize
What he was.

At last my father said,
'Yes.'
And I
Became Mixcoatl's wife.
He was a warrior,
But he was good.
I could see his spirit

And
It was white
As the shadow of the Creator,
He was good,
My heart and my spirit
Belonged to him,
I was happy.

We left my village and
went to
The Chichimeca camp,
In the north.

We could not have each other
Till the marriage
Had been consecrated by
His brothers.

His brothers refused.
They said
They would conquer all of Mexico
And
Girls like me
Would become their slaves.
They said
We would clean their filth
And
Eat their trash
And
At night
We would sleep at their feet.

Mixcoatl became outraged.
I told him
' No!'
But
He drew his war axe
And fought

It was a terrible fight.

        Mixcoatl fought like
        A wild animal,
        Like a Jaguar.
        His axe swung in all directions,
        and men fell before him
        Like leaves in a whirlwind.

        Then
        An arrow struck him
        In his chest,
        And yet more arrows came,
        And Mixcoatl fell
        Into the shadows.

        His last words sounded
        like a prayer---
        'Run!'
        He said.
        And I rushed off
        Into the darkness.

The last I saw of my husband
        was
        The two fingers of his left hand
        Separated in the shape of a "V".

        I ran
        And hid.
        The Chichimecas
        Were always near.
        Somehow,
        By some strange source
        I was not caught.
        On I traveled,
        Sleeping
        In the branches of trees
        In the daytime

And
Traveling at night.

Each village I would reach
      Had already been visited
      By the Chichimecas,
      Already destroyed
      And
      The sign of their God
      Was left behind.
      Tezcatlipoca
      Had been there.
      Tezcatlipoca,
      The dark lord
      Of human sacrifice.

When I reached my home,
      My father's village,
      I found the whole town
      Destroyed
      And
      Everyone dead
      And
      Branded with the sign of
      Tezcatlipoca.
      Their hearts were gone,
      And
      The right foot
      Of each Holy Man
      Had been stolen.

I left there and
      Thought to come here.
      But instead
      I became lost
      And
      Found myself at Chapultepec
      (Hill of the Grasshopper)

I tried to go
To the lake for water
But I
Fell into the mud.
I
Became stuck there.
I turned
And tried to move
But I was fast.

It was dark.

A strange thing happened.
People were coming toward me,
I thought they were Chichimecas
Come to kill me,
But
They were not.
They were
People from the future.
They carried a great cactus
And
A serpent
And
They were weeping
Because they had lost
Their eagle.
They came to me
And talked.
They told me
They were servants
Of the
"Lord of the Dawn"
And that
They loved me,
They had to help me.

An old lady with white hair
Came forward then

And
Wiped my face
And called me
Earth Mother
And
Dawn Child,
She said
I was covered with beauty.

Then all of the stars
Turned green in the sky,
Green as jade.
And
One very bright star
Fell from the sky,
Stopped above my stomach,
Glowed very bright.
Then
Entered my stomach
Through my womb,
And
I fell to sleep.

I had no dream,
Not really,
Only a feeling of
Great contentment
And joy.

When I awoke the old white haired woman
Was still there near me,
She spoke,
' Mixcoatl is waiting for you
Beyond the Morning Star,
He is waiting,
Hurry and have the baby,
He is waiting for you. '

She stood up and
Walked away.
She said no more.

Now
I am here
At Xochicalco
with all of you
And my dear uncle Salavi.
I have no husband,
But I know
I will soon have a baby."

"Yes,"
Said Salavi,
"The child will be born
          In the ninth moon,
          Always in the ninth moon
On the day of One Reed,
In the year of One Reed---
In the ninth moon."

And the old priests of Xochicalco
          All sighed together,

     "Grandfather
      Grandfather
      Grandfather
      Grandfather."

They wept,
They knew it was true,
"The Lord of the Dawn"
Was coming.

THE VISION OF SALAVI

Salavi left the Temple of Quetzalcoatl
        And went into the barracks
        of the Nonoalca
        And chose twenty of them
        To go forth into all parts
        Of the land,
        To the extent of all directions
        And to tell
        Everyone they encountered
        That
        He would soon be on Earth.

He reminded them that
        No one will believe you.
        "That
        Is exactly as it is meant to be."
        Salavi laughed.
        "But
        Tell them anyway,
        Tell them once more,
        Then
        Tell them they have been told---
        And
        Leave---"

Salavi then returned to
        The Temple of the Dawn
        And prepared for
        A vision.

        Four days he fasted in the Temple,
        No food
        No water
        No words from his lips
        No sleep.

Then
He rested
Slept for a full night
Arose in the morning before the sunlight
Ate raw fruit
Drank of the cactus tea
Drank of Water.

He cried for the vision.
His song was heard throughout the city.
And all who heard
Knew why.
No one understood the words
To the Ancient Chant.
Those words, and
That song
Were said to
Have come from another world.
A world now buried beneath
The rolling tides of salt water
In the
Great Eastern Sea,
And now known only by
The elders of the
Council of Quetzalcoatl.

"Evoke the nether world,
Evoke the spirit of the Earth Mother,
The voice of the Clouds,
Evoke the Heart of Heaven
And
The Heart of the Earth,
And quest for the hidden words."

Salavi's vision came from
An ancient tree.
A tree
He had never seen

But
Had often heard about.

The vision came
Through the branches
Of the tree
And
He wondered
If this could be
The "Tree of Life."

The answer came back
"Yes."

He questioned
Of Mixcoatl
And the Chichimeca.
The answer
Came from the roots of the Great Tree,
Came to him
In this way.

"The Chichimeca are as much a part of this story
As is
The Feathered Serpent.
Without them
The Manifestation
Would not be true,
Would not be complete.

The Chichimeca are
From a faraway land
On the other side of your Earth-land,
On the other side of your Earth-mother,
And they,
Like you
Are very important
To the Creation of All Things.

Chichimeca
means
People of Dog Lineage,
Descendant of a man called Dog.
This man
Was a most important
servant of the Creation
In another time,
And they,
The Chichimeca
Are his descendants.

Mixcoatl was
Their Gifted One,
The last
Of their seed.
He
Is the Burning Bush
Of This Land.

Mixcoatl,
Cloud Serpent,
Milky Way,
The
Tree of the Sky,
You can be sure that
He was faithful
To his very death."

The vision became bright now, and continued .
"Tezcatlepoca is not a Chichimeca idea,
He belongs to your people.
If
He is blood thirsty
That is because
The people want blood,
He is a God
An idol

A creation of man.
He comes
From
Your choice of
The first two heavens.

Know him well,
Learn his habits,
Learn his power,
Because
Man
Has created him
And
He
Will be here
Until
The end of the Ninth Hell.
Then
He will remove his mask
And
You will be surprised
Who
He really is."

The vision had passed.

The Little People,

      The Pockwatchies
      And the Tlaloques
      Danced
      From hill to hill,
      Down
      Every moon-bathed path they went,
      Singing a new song,
      One never heard before,
      Not even by them.
      On and on they went

Through woods
And over desert,
Singing as they danced.

The Pockwatchies,
The Little People
Were thrilled with the news of
Fulfillment.
They carried the news
From hill to hill
From wood to wood.
In their tiny hearts they knew what was coming.
These
Little guardians of the Earth
Knew
That one day
They
Would have to face
The brunt of man's ignorance,
Yet
They danced on
Regardless,
Laughing
And singing
Of the wonders of the Creator,
For they knew that

All things that must be
Must be in balance
And
That takes practice.

THE DAWN CHILD PROPHECY

"It's a boy!"
Cried the children.
"It's a boy!"
The word was carried
By the children
From
House to House
Of Xochicalco.

The child
was greeted
With
Great excitement.
He is born,
They said.

The excitement
Turned
To wonderment,
And a
Sort of despair
When
The news came forth. . . .
Chimalma,
She who walked in beauty,
Has passed
Into
The world of the dead,
Has returned
To her Earth Mother,
Her
Spirit
Has gone.

She
Has borne

The Sacred One,
Now
She
Has passed through
The gates
Of
The other world.

She is now
With Mixcoatl
In
The land of green light,
Beyond
The Morning Star.
Chimalma
Had
Given birth
To the long-awaited
Dawn Child,
And
As the prophecy
Had predicted
She died.
Her funeral was simple.
A grave
Within the temple walls.
On the grave
Was placed a
Dead bough
Of an old tree.

The baby boy arrived on Earth
On the
Day One Reed,
In the
Year One Reed,
Exactly as
The prophecy said.

The Sacred Tablets told
    Of His birthday
    And
    Laid out a
    Tentative description
    Of His life.

    Those Tablets
    Went further
    To describe
    That this
    Entire epic,
    Which
    Was now
    Taking place
    Was but
    a fragment
    Of what was yet
    To come.

The Sacred Tablets,
    So faithfully guarded
    By the
    Council of Quetzalcoatl
    Predicted the future
    Of
    The entire continent.
    It was not a
    Vague prophecy,
    But rather
    One of
    Eminent magnitude.

Using the Fifty-two year cycle
    Of the
    Sacred Astronomical Calendar
    Of
    Ancient Mexico

As
Its
Exacting catalyst,
And
Defining
A number of check points
Within its
1144 year periods,
It formulated
A prophecy
Unlike any other prophecy
Of mankind.
Its matrix
Lay hidden
In the shadows
Of
The lowland jungles,
All but
Lost in time,
Save
For the
Sacred Tablets
Held by the
Council of Quetzalcoatl.

These Tablets
prophecied
The coming events
Of the Americas,
Both
Land and people,
And did this
In a
Series of symbolic Heavens
Thirteen all told,
and
Nine Hells,
An accumulation

of twenty-two cycles
Of the
Fifty-two year calendar
Twenty-two times Fifty-two
Eleven hundred forty-four years.

The First Heaven
Had been entered
One hundred four years
Before
The birth
Of
The Lord of the Dawn.

In other words,
Two heavens
Had been spent
And the
First checkpoint
Had been
Arrived at
Upon the birth
Of the child
On the
Day One Reed
And the
Year One Reed.
This
Confirmed
In the minds
Of the believers
The accuracy
Of the prophecy

Ce Acatl is the Nahuatl name
For
One Reed.

Topiltzin is also a Nahuatl word
　　　　　Meaning
　　　　　Our Lord
　　　　　Or
　　　　　Our Prince,
　　　　　Thus,
　　　　　The child's calendar name
　　　　　Was
　　　　　"Ce Acatl Topiltzin Quetzalcoatl"
　　　　　In English
　　　　　"Our Lord One Reed Feathered Serpent".
　　　　　And He was
　　　　　The long-awaited
　　　　　Lord of the Dawn.

Ce Acatl's infancy was spent
　　　　　In the
　　　　　Temples of Xochicalco,
　　　　　Raised by
　　　　　The Temple Virgins,
　　　　　Loved and protected
　　　　　by all.

When he was quite young he
　　　　　Was taken
　　　　　To the
　　　　　Valley of the Moon
　　　　　Where
　　　　　He spent the rest
　　　　　Of his childhood,
　　　　　Returning to Xochicalco
　　　　　On occasion
　　　　　To take part in
　　　　　Holy days
　　　　　And certain ceremonies.

In the Valley of the Moon
　　　　　He played
　　　　　And lived
　　　　　The life
　　　　　Of any child.

Perhaps the only life
  He ever had
  That
  Really belonged
  To himself.
  There
  He realized
  The creation,
  The little brooks
  became
  His song
  And
  He talked
  To the old trees,
  Rolled in the deep grass
  And
  Whistled to the birds.

  He
  Became a friend
  To all the things
  Of
  The Valley of the Moon,
  Especially
  The Little People
  Who became
  His constant companions
  and
  One of them
  Known as Quill
  Became his teacher,
  Recalled to Ce Acatl
  The romance
  Of the Clouds and the Earth,
  Told him
  Of the
  Birth of life

And
Of the
Creation of the Little People,
Told him of
Two Lord and Two Lady
And
Their twins.
He asked if
Ce Acatl had a twin.
Ce Acatl said,
"Yes."
(But that's
another story)

Ce Acatl thought
Of the "Tree of Life"
And knew
Its importance
And
More than once
The thought
Came to him,
"How much alike
Is
The story of
The Clouds and the Earth,
And
My Mother and Father,
Only
The Earth didn't die."

He wondered
If
One day the Earth Mother
Would die,
And
His first prayer
At sunrise
Was always that
She wouldn't.

Salavi's death brought Ce Acatl
    From the
    Valley of the Moon.
    He returned
    To his valley
    Many times,
    But
    only to visit.

Once Salavi was dead
    Ce Acatl's life
    Became
    The property of
    All of Mexico.

    He
    Was nine years old.

    They say
    He tore the mask
    From
    The Feathered Serpent
    Of Xochicalco.

    They say
    He purified the
    Story of Creation.

    They say
    He fasted twenty days
    and
    Spoke to the dead
    Of Teotihuacan

    They say
    He went to Oaxaca
    And
    Talked to the Tree of Life.

They say
He met his twin
In Oaxaca.

They say
They, the twins,
meditated for forty days and nights.

They say
Their spiritual power
Was
So great
That
The womb of the Earth
Glowed for four years.

They say
He journeyed
To the World of the dead
To speak once more
With Salavi.

They say
Many things
Of this boy.
And
Always
Shall say even more.

Salavi was buried under
A
Tall spruce tree.
His flesh
Became a tear
Of
The Earth Mother,
Became
A spring.

And the spring
Is always
Known as
Charm Springs
And
Wanders all over
The earth.
Those
Who drink
Of its water
Will
Always be reminded
Of
Old Salavi,
A forerunner
of
The Lord of the Dawn.

THE MORNING STAR YOUTH

The Morning Star was
Bright in the heavens
When
Ce Acatl made
His decision
to go to the camp
Of the Chichimeca
And
Bring his father's bones back,
And to bury them
Beside
The grave of his mother.

So,
He went.

Mixcoatl's brother lured Ce Acatl,
who was now twenty years old,
On to a mountain top
To talk,
He said.
The brother
Was
A great warrior
And knew
He could
Kill
Ce Acatl
With
His bare hands.

Lightning flashed
From
The cloudless sky
And
The evil brother
Was hurled
Into the world of the dead.

Ce Acatl
Returned to Xochicalco
With
His father's remains,
Dug the grave
Himself
Beside the grave
Of his mother,
Still marked
With the dead branch
Of
The ancient tree.

When
Mixcoatl's grave
Was closed
Ce Acatl
Said
A short prayer.
"There
Is no remover of difficulties
Other than
The Creator,
And
We all abide
By His bidding.
We
Are all his servants."
And
The dead branch
Turned green.

THE DIVINE RULER

Due to the death of Mixcoatl's brother,
Ce Acatl
Became the Emperor
Of the Chichimeca.

He first pacified them
With Hikuli
A divine cactus
With
No thorns.

"The cactus will not
Hurt you,"
He said,
"It has no thorns,

The cactus
Is a
Spirit medicine
That is meant
To bring back peace to your dreams,
Calm to your waking hours,
And
Purpose to your life!
Take it
And
Be reminded
That it is a part of
Your Earth Mother's spirit,
Not to be toyed with,
Not to be
Made
A god."

Tezcatlipoca and his secret society that
    Now hid in shadows,
    Waited
    And laid their plans
    For
    The destruction of
    Ce Acatl's
    New
    Way of life,
    A
    Sort of
    Great Peace.

Now Ce Acatl called upon
    The Nonoalca,
    And
    The Amanteca
    At the Temple of Xochicalco.

The Nonoalca were of Zapotec,
Mazatec decent
And
The Amanteca were master artists,
Descendants of the Teotihuacan people
Who
In their past had built
The Pyramids of the Sun
And
The Moon,
And designed
The Temple of Butterflies
On the
Road of the Dead
In Teotihuacan
And
Had   covered
The Temple of the Butterflies
With images
Of the Little People.
The Nonoalca
Were
Mathematicians,
Philosophers
And Astronomers,
They had also
Mastered the
Art of casting gold.

Combining the skill of these ancient cultured people
With the vitality
Of the Chichimeca
Ce Acatl
Brought into clear focus
A new renaissance
Which flowered into
The
Jewel of Ancient Mexico

And
It's heart
Was in the
City of Wonder
Known as
Tollan.
The people
of Tollan
Became known as
The Toltec.

Tollan was the capital of the empire
Of empires.
Seldom, if ever,
Rivaled
In the world.
Tollan
Was the heart
Of all
That had ever been
Good and pure
In
This ancient land.
It was the
Essence of grandeur,
The apex of prosperity.
Tollan
Was pure spirit
Manifested
In works of stone and feather,
gold and jade.
It was a world
Of religious splendor
And
Godly fulfillment.
A sample
Of
What man
Could do

With
Peace.

They say
Corn grew the size of a man,
Each cob the size of a man.

They say
Cotton grew in many colors,
Red, green, blue, violet, turquoise
and Yellow,
Earth colors of tan, black, brown
And a pale orange.

They say
Fountains of pure water
Flowed through the city
And
That this water
Was brought from the
Very heart
Of the Earth.
They say
Cocoa trees grew throughout the city,
Vines of orchids
And vanilla, avocado and mangoes.

They say
Birds of many colors
And sizes
Lived
With the people of Tollan.

They say
The people of Tollan
Were
The most beautiful people
In all the world,
Because of what

They had done,
Because
They had learned
The secret of
Peace was:
The unity of all things.

But strangely
They began to
Forget What
They had been taught.
They say this was the
secret work of Tezcatlipoca
and the Jaguar societies,

They say,
The Toltecs,
The people of Tollan
Believing lies
Made a toy
Of the thornless cactus,
The Hikuli
And
Used it
As the sacrament
Of their God
Tezcatlipoca.

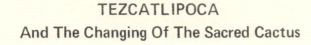

TEZCATLIPOCA
And The Changing Of The Sacred Cactus

In the olden days,
>In the days before
>The beginning
>Of the
>Thirteen Heavens,
>Tezcatlipoca
>Was not
>An evil god.
>According to stories,
>He once ruled the
>People of the Earth.
>He
>Was
>The Lord of Fire,
>And
>Prince of feasts.
>He
>Ruled the night sky,
>Thus
>He was known
>As the
>"Dark Lord of the North."

Long, Long ago he had been
>A Gifted One,
>They say
>He had come to Earth
>Directly from
>The Creator,
>And,
>Here on Earth
>He had done
>Many wonderful things.
>When he left
>He told the people

Of a new and wonderful prophet
That would come and visit them
He told them,
When that day comes
They should listen to the New Words.

Through the endless times that followed
His philosophy
Of Peace
And
Of Love
Lost its place in the
Minds of men.
His potency was gone,
His philosophy forgotten,
His purpose in coming changed,
Changed
To meet the desires of men,
Rather than
The desires of the Creator.

Now, with the Chichimeca,
He was reduced
To
The size of a
Bloodthirsty monster,
Who
Devoured human Hearts,
And
Destroyed stars in the sky
So
The Sun
Would not have to
Fight
With them
At Sunrise.

As surely as the ignorance of man
Was reflected

Upon the
Once beautiful philosophy
Of Tezcatlipoca,
So
Was it reflected upon
The once sensible
Use of Hikuli.

Hikuli was once the
Holy Sacrament
Of a Gifted One.
Its story goes back
Long, long before
Tezcatlipoca.
It was still the
Sacred brew of the
Temples
At the time
Of the Chichimeca migration
Into the
Valley of Mexico.

Now, it was used by fools,
Who thought
They could rule
The minds of man,
Thus
Rule the Earth.

Hikuli
Became the blinding light
That
Led the victims
To the top of the pyramid
To have their hearts
Ripped from their bodies,
In a horrible ceremony
Dedicated to
Tezcatlipoca.

Tezcatlipoca grew very large, very fast.
Now,
The Toltec,
The "new people",
Had everything,
And
Wanted more.
They
Scorned
The teachings of
Ce Acatl
Scorned the presence
Of the Nonoalca
And
The Amanteca.

The "New People" became drunk and conceited
With power and glory.
They
Brought forth images
Of their
Dark Lord
Of human sacrifice,
Tezcatlipoca,
And
Slowly began
To build the
Nightmare of the future,
War. . .,
Conquest. . .,
And Gods.

THE FALL OF TOLLAN

Tollan started to crack
    And decay
    From within.
    Grim
    Were the faces
    Of the Nonoalca,
    Who
    Knew the prophecy
    Of
    The Lord of the Dawn.

"Now we will see our work,
    Our labor
    Wasted,"

    They said.
    "It is not wasted,"
    Said Ce Acatl,
    "You will see,
    Not one drop of sweat
    Was wasted here.
    You and I and
    The Toltec
    Have made something known here
    At Tollan.
    But, now,
    Our work is done. . . .
    Well, almost done.

One last gift I have for you
    Before I leave. . . ,"
    He said to
    The Toltecs.
    "At noon tomorrow
    Come to
    My Temple
    And
    I will give it to you.

Bring
Tezcatlipoca
So he may
Take part in
This
Gift of Gifts.''

At noon of the next day
    The Toltecs
    Swarmed around
    Ce Acatl's
    Temple.
    So used were they
    To
    Receiving
    That they
    Had come to think
    It common,
    Rather than
    A gift.
    Many jeers came from the crowd,
    Laughter
    And mockery.

At the foot of Ce Acatl's Temple
    Was placed
    A great image of
    Tezcatlipoca,
    The Dark Lord of the North.

Ce Acatl Topiltzin Quetzalcoatl
    Walked down
    The great steps of
    The pyramid
    To the
    Stone statute of
    Tezcatlipoca.
    He smiled and said,
    ''My Brother!

And you,
The Toltec,
You are also
My brothers and
My sisters."

Now, a hush fell over the crowd,
The sun
Seemed
To dim
In the sky.

"Fear not," said Ce Acatl.
"No harm will come
To you
This day.
You
Are as safe as
If in my Mother's homeland.
You cannot even hurt
Yourself
At this moment.

My people," he continued,
"You,
Wonderful,
Wonderful
Children.
I love you.
You are surely
The soul of the Earth.
You have not
Failed me in one way,
Nor
Will you ever.
Understand
What I am saying here,
For that is of importance.
Understand,
I did not try to be

Your Lord,
Nor
Did you try to be my people,
Nor
Did we try to build Tollan,
Understand
That all of this is senseless
Unless
It serves a greater purpose.

One day, a long time from now
    In the days of
    The Seventh Hell
    A man
    Or a boy
    Or a woman
    Or a girl
    Will come to you
    And
    They will say,
    'Behold the Tree of Life,'
    Because
    As surely as you cast me out
    Of your city with scorn,
    You may not
    Cast out the
    'Tree of Life.'

Ce Acatl then held up a large Hikuli
    In his right hand.
    With his foot
    He dug a small hole
    In the Earth.
    "Now, watch," he said,
    as he placed
    The cactus
    In the hole.
    He stepped back

and
Looking at the sun
He spoke these words.
"Lord of the Dawn
Royal Seal of Eternal Life
Caster of Truths
Master of Cosmic Force
Creator of Time and Light
Giver of matter,
Touch this place."

He turned and walked back
Up the stairs
Of the pyramid.
"Fake!"
Someone shouted.
"Fake!
Liar
Sinner
Fake! "
Eater of filth
Devourer of human hearts,
Fake
Sinner
Liar
Eater of human flesh
Liar
Fake
Eater of human hearts
Devourer of human flesh."

But Hikuli became bitter,
So foul was it
That it made
People vomit.
No longer was it
A
Pleasant food.

Its name was now

   Peyote

   And

   It was like

   An uncontrollable Father,

   A Dark God.

   Cotton

   Grew in white only,

   Corn was corn only,

   White and yellow and sweet.

   The fountains went dry.

   The orchids

   Could not be grown,

   nor vanilla,

   Nor avocado,

   Nor mangoes.

   The

   Birds left.

And where Ce Acatl had placed

   The Hikuli

   a

   Tree of Thorns grew,

   And

   The strange forbidding tree

   Refused to die,

   It was created out of man's desire,

   And

   Insisted on living.

   All the cocoa trees

   Of Tollan

   Turned into

   Beautiful Thorn Bushes.

But the People, the Toltec, had
    What they wanted.
    They had
    Tezcatlipoca,
    The god of
    Human sacrifice.
    And Tezcatlipoca would write
    The history
    Of the Toltec
    And
    The people
    To follow the Toltec.

But at the end of the Ninth Hell
    Tezcatlipoca
    Would take off his mask
    And
    They would be surprised
    To learn
    Who he really is.

THE MARCH TO THE SOUTH

"Tezcatlipoca has driven
      Quetzalcoatl
      Away!
      Quetzalcoatl
      Fell to sin!
      Tezcatlipoca
      Defeated
      Quetzalcoatl!
      Quetzalcoatl
      Was not true!
      He did not do as he said!
      He lied!"

Those were the words
> Of the Toltec lords
> Who followed
> Ce Acatl,
> But,
> In the Sacred Temple
> Of Chamala,
> in Tollan,
> Some people,
> From time to time, came,
> And,
> Looking up at the
> Feathered Serpent on the wall,
> All that was left
> Of His sign at Tollan,
> They would pray.
> They would say
> *"Forgive!"*

Ce Acatl and his Nonoalca and Amanteca followers
> had left Tollan
> And traveled south.
> They
> Reached
> The valley of Mexico
> And
> Lake
> Tezcoco
> Where
> long ago
> The lovely Chimalma
> Had
> Received the Seed.
> Ce Acatl stopped there
> For many days
> And prayed.

Then on they went to the foot
Of the great Volcano,
To the famous
Popocatepetl.
There
His followers stopped
And
Made camp for awhile.
This
Was regarded
As the golden days
To Ce Acatl.

While he was there he told
The children
Many stories
At night,
By the blazing fire.
Told them stories
Of the
"Little People"
And
of Quill his
Pockwatchie teacher
And
Recalled many dreams
He had,
Long ago
In the
Valley of the Moon.

Here at the foot of the great volcano
Ce Acatl
roamed
Through the hills.
Once again
He sang with the brook
And whistled
To the bird,
Rolled in the deep grass

And returned for a moment
To the love of his childhood.

It is said that Quill returned to him
And that
The two of them
Smoked tobacco together
At an old pine tree stump
and Laughed
About the olden days.

Ce Acatl found these days to be sweet
As honey
And
Filled
With a thousand memories
He
Had forgotten
During
The sacrifice of Tollan.

The fresh snow water
And the
Clear mountain air
Was good for the whole tribe.
Deer meat
And
Autumn mushrooms,
Berries from the hollows,
And the
Fragrance of juniper fires
Transformed the camp-sight
into a natural shrine
Of human friendship.
Ce Acatl commented
That the glories of Tollan
Could never compare
With the least of the Creator's
wild lands,

And he said,
"The wealth that men die for
If only they knew,
Is but the corruptions
Of their own creations.
The real gift,
The gift a child can
Accept and love,
These solitudes of nature
With those you love,
Are as close as man
Can come to
What
He has in
His master plan."

Popocatepetl now loomed up before them.
Threatening smoke belched
From the mountain crater
And
Low rumbles came from the living stone.
The earth trembled
As the tribe climbed between
Popocatepetl and Ixtaccihuatl (the
Sleeping Lady) following a
prophecy,
Upward through the dense forest
Of the ever steepening slopes
Of the volcano.

More than two thirds of the tribe
was lost on the Mountain.
Fell to a blinding snow storm
High above the timber line,

Some
Were caught in
An avalanche
And swept away.

Others
Froze to death
During
The fireless nights
On the
Volcano of Death.
In a glen on the eastern slope
Of the mountain
Ce Acatl
At last sat
And wept
For
His lost companions,
He fasted
And meditated,
Prayed
And offered votives
In
Their memories.
Four
Men
Wandered into the camp
In this glen
And stayed awhile.
To talk.
These
Were four Holy Men
From
Four different directions.
Ce Acatl
Seemed to know them.
Each man spent
A day
In solitude with
Ce Acatl.
At the end,
Of the fourth day
Ce Acatl
Called the

remaining of the tribe
Together
And with the
Four Holy Men
He told them
What
Had happened
And
What this meant.

"It was prophecied," he started,
　　"That these
　　Four men
　　Would find us here.
　　They are all
　　Holy Men.
　　All four of them
　　Know
　　Who they are
　　And
　　Why
　　They are here.

I have given each of them
　　Four words
　　To
　　Take Back
　　To their peoples
　　And to
　　put into
　　Their ceremonies
　　So
　　It will not be forgotten.

But one of these four words
　　Were commonly given
　　To each
　　Of the Holy Men.

I
Give
That Word
To
All of you now,
The word is
'Tree'.
Use it.
By the sign of the Tree
You
Will know
Each
And
Every
Manifestation
In this world.
All
Manifestations
are good,
None
Better than the other,
All
Are related
All
Are meant
To do
A part of
The Master Work.
Do not look
For miracles,
They will come.
Look
For the 'Tree'
And
Never,
Never
Forget it.

Now I say farewell to you.

I

Must leave

You

Here.

You know my teachings,

You know the prophecy.

One

Of these four men

Will go

With you.

It is this one,

The oldest,

The man with a beard,

His name is

Gucumatz.

Follow him

As if

He were me.

And the other three men

They too are me,

And

I have given

Each of them

Part

Of my spirit.

Remember

'The Tree.'

Now I leave you and

If you ask

'To where?'

I will answer

'To the Tree of Life,'

To the world of my twin,

To the land of Eight Deer

To my Zapotec homeland.' "

And

Ce Acatl Topiltzin

Left

And went to
Oaxaca,
To
The Valley of the Tree.

THE VALLEY OF THE TREE

During a terrible thunderstorm
It is said
Ce Acatl
Spent a night
With a
Huiteca family.
They fed him
And
Played music for him.
The father,
A strong Indian farmer
Showed Ce Acatl

A stone carving
He had and
Told him:

*"This carving
Tells of
The coming of the
Lord of the Dawn.
It says
He will come
In the
Year One Reed.
It says
He will build a city
and
Change the world."*

The farmer had no idea who
He was talking to.
He continued.
"Now," he said,
*"Many people say
He will not come.
Many people say
It is a long time from now
That he will come.
Some people say
He will come from the East
And
He will bring a great book
Of words and numbers.
Other people say
He will come
From a tree
And
Count the
Last Twenty days
Of the Creation.*

What
Do you say
About this?"

Ce Acatl grew grey with the depth
of his answer.
"If
I told you
Of my thought,
Of what I know
Of the Spirit
Of the Lord of the Dawn,
If I told you
Of what
I think will happen.
You would laugh
And think me crazy.

"So I say this only:
One day
A race
Shall walk upon this earth,
A race of men
Whose spirits
Are so great,
Whose wisdom
Is so complete,
Whose powers
To commune with the Creator
Are
So keen
They will dwarf
The doings
Of
The Lord of the Dawn
Of our day.
When that day comes
The Creator
Will send forth

A
Manifestation
That will
In turn
Amaze the wisest men
Of that
Unbelievable age.
And even then
The greatest brains on earth
Will wonder---
Has he come?
Will he come?
Or
Has he been here?"

In this way Ce Acatl traveled
through the countryside.
Meeting people,
Staying overnight
In their homes,
Teaching
And
Leaving.
Only to find another house,
A village
Or
A lonely soul
wandering through life alone

Till at last he reached the
"Valley of the Tree."
His sandals were worn out,
His clothing bleached
From the mountain sun
His beard
Had turned grey
And
His back
Was growing weak,

He walked now
With a staff.

Through the valley he passed
       unnoticed
       As the
       Lord of the Dawn.
       Yet
       The thoughtful
       Zapotec people
       Made him feel
       Oaxaca
       Was his home.
       "Welcome old-man,"
       They said.
       "Welcome Grandfather!
       Eat and sleep,
       Rest and
       Tell us of your journey."

But Ce Acatl spoke not,
       And rested only
       At springs,
       Ate the food of the field
       And
       Carried On
       Toward the "great Tree"

Ce Acatl was forty-six when he reached
       The Valley of the Tree.
       This is not thought old
       In our time,
       But, in those days
       People died of old age
       At thirty-five
       And few lived to be forty.
       Most graves were of people
       Less than
       Twenty years of age.

It was late one evening
When he at last
Reached
The Great Tree.
He could see it
For miles away
And
His approach
Was slow.
The Tree
Seemed to glow
With
An ever brightening aura,
Green in color
Like transparent jade.

At last he reached the
Great Tree,
And fell
Upon the roots,
Exhausted.

There he slept and dreamed.
When he awoke
He found
He
Was surrounded
By people,
All of them
Reflected holiness,
All
Were dressed in white,
Wearing necklaces of clay
Made
In the form of
The Circle
And the Cross.

At last an old priest
Of their clan
Came forward.
"I
Know who you are,"
He said.
"We
Have been waiting for you."
Then
Very shyly he added:
"Welcome!
Welcome home my Lord!"
And like a burst of light
In a dark cave
The entire crowd
swarmed around him
And
Showered him
With such love as
He had never known before.

Everyone had to touch him
Or
He had to touch them.
Mothers
Brought their babies,
The
Children
Brought their dogs
And pet animals
And birds
For the
Lord of the Dawn to touch.
Laughter and excitement resounded
Through the Valley.
Dancing
And singing,
And merriment
Were
Everywhere.

The celebration went on
    For days,
    Perhaps weeks.
    The
    Lord of the Dawn
    Had
    Come home.

"And my twin?" Ce Acatl asked.
    "Too late,
    Years ago he was sacrificed
    On the Sacred Mountain
    By
    The Jaguar Priests.
    He was sacrificed
    With his lover,
    Two Turquoise.
    He had traveled
    Into
    The Nine Hells
    And
    Brought back a
    Message
    Of the future.

    He
    was faithful
    to
    Your cause
    Till the end."
"Of course he was," said Ce Acatl,
    "But
    It is
    Our Cause!"

Ce Acatl was given the news
    Of the Nonoalca
    And Gucumatz.

They
Had built a
Great pyramid
At the town
Of Cholula,
Given the word
And left.
They
Had gone on to
Yucatan
And
Were now building
A
New
Tollan.
They called the place
Chichen-Itza.

And a whole new era is coming about.
A great confederacy
Of
All the Maya
And Toltec tribes
Is
Being formed.
They say
The confederacy
Is based on
The
Philosophy of
The "Tree."

"It is good to hear these words
Of Our Cause,"
Said Ce Acatl.
"But I have little time
Left to talk.
Time is running out,
My cycle will soon close,
And
We have our greatest work

Laid

Out for us."

Ce Acatl resigned himself

To live under

The ancient Tree

And to work from

The Tree.

For four years

He

Did so.

There, under the Tree,

He designed

The

Sacred Tree of Mitla,

And called it a

Library,

The House of Books.

"This," he said, *"is a monument*

To the Tree of Life,

To

The whole Creation.

The city

Will be like a Tree,

Half above the Earth,

Half below the Earth,

The trunk

And

The roots.

The roots will be the

Tombs of our dead.

The artist,

Poet,

Writers of books,

The Librarians

Who

Will be the

Great Seers
Readers of all books,
They too shall be
Tombed
In the roots.

As the roots of a tree reaches
Down into the past,
So
The roots of this Library,
Will Reach
Into its own past.
Mitla
Will be like
a
Stone Tree.

Above the surface
Will stand the temples,
The Library itself.
And it,
Like a tree,
Will reflect
What it
Has been subjected to
By the
Natural forces.

Wind rising, rain falling,
Sun rising, sun falling,
Clouds rising, lightning falling,
Life rising, death falling,
Tide rising, tide falling,
Man rising, man falling,
Tree of Life rising, rising, rising.

The Library,
The house of books
Came to be

Exactly as
He
Had designed it.
It was built
At the
Womb of the Earth,
At the
Cave
Of the Nether World.

And the Temples of Mitla are unique
In the
World of
Architectural design,
The
Epitome
Of
Zapotec-Mixtec Art.
Every stone
Was cut
By human hands.
Perfectly in balance
With
All things,
And done by
People who
Knew that
This
Was far more
Than a building.

The question has often been asked,
Who
Built
The Temples of Mitla?

It was designed by the
Lord of the Dawn,
And built
By people
Who loved
And
Who followed
Him!

It was done, but Ce Acatl
Never saw
The Temple completed.
He had come
From the
Dawn of the Third Heaven
And
Stayed a while,
Stayed fifty-two years
And
Left.
Gone to his
Mother's homeland,
To the
Land of the Black and the Red.

He, Ce Acatl Topiltzin, had come
Out of the Black,
The darkness of
Man's mind,
entered into
The Red World of the Sun,
And had returned,
Knowing
More than all others
For
He had penetrated
The world of time and
Completed a cycle set forth

In another creation
long, long ago,
and far,
Ever so far away.

Four years he had spent under
The most ancient Tree.
There
He had designed the
Library,
At the
Womb of the Earth Mother.
Designed a Library
Like a
Sacred City
And that City
Became known as
Mitla,
City of the Dead.

Ce Acatl was fifty-two years old
When he died.
One short cycle
Of the Sacred Calendar,
One
Of the Lord of Life's
Thirteen Heavens
Was all the time
He
Was given.

The date of his birth by the Christian Calendar
Was
947 AD,
His departure
999AD.

And Ce Acatl Topiltzin Quetzalcoatl,
The
Lord of the Dawn
Departed
Into the
World of the Dead,
To the Underworld,
To Mitla.
There he rested,

And
Waited,
And
Waited.

It is said the sun disappeared
From the sky
When
He passed.
It is said
The birds
Stopped singing
And that a
Hush fell
Over the entire planet.
And
Burning bright
In the heavens
Directly above
The great tree,
The Tree of Life,
Glowed
The planet Venus,
The
Morning Star.

The march to the south
Was done!

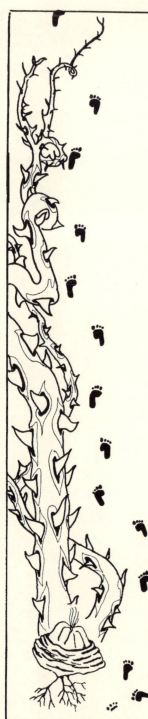

THE SACRIFICE

Now they came,

> Leaping from the rocks,
> Springing from the trees,
> From the placid water.
> Now they come
> Dancing,
> Whirling,
> Spinning
> And
> Sliding.
> Through the
> Radiant colors of nature,
> From grains of sand
> And
> Leaves of grass,
> From flowers
> And cactus,
> They came.
> The guardians of the
> Earth Mother,
> The Little People,
> Singing their song
> With
> Their knowledge.

Sad at first, with the parting
  Of their friend,
  But
  Quickly returning
  To joy
  With the realization
  Of what was coming.
  The greatest adventure
  Was
  Just beyond
  The horizon
  And the tiny
  Earth spirits knew
  It was there.

They watched the history unfold
  Before their little eyes.
  From their hiding places
  They saw,
  They heard,
  and
  They kept close count
  Of the
  Thirteen Heavens.

As had been prophesied
  They saw Tollan,
  The Emerald of Mexico
  Fall
  And
  Weather
  Like bones in the Sun.

And the Aztecs came,
  As wild nomads
  From the north.
  Came
  From the
  Same land

As the Chichemeca before them
And,

As prophesied,

Lived for awhile

On the mud flats

Of Lake Tezcoco,

The very place

Where once

Chamalma

Received the Seed.

They moved

To the man-made island

In the lake,

And

Built their

City of wonder.

They called it

Tenochtitlan.

The Aztec

had been brought

To Lake Tezcoco

By the vision of

One of their people,

An old, white haired woman,

A sort of prophetess.

And the Aztec

Used as

Their symbol

The elements of

Her vision.

The Serpent---The past

The Cactus---The "Tree of Thorns"

The Eagle---The Sun.

And the "Little People"

Heard the ghastly philosophy

Of the Aztecs,

Who believed themselves

To be the chosen people of

the Sun
And
Like all chosen people,
They became lost.
They believed
The Sun was God,
A great Eagle.

The Sun is a warrior,
Said the Aztec Lord,
The Sun must
Fight the stars
From the sky
At every dawn.

We, the Aztec, are sent
To Earth
To feed the Sun,
To strengthen him
So He can continue
His fight against
The stars.

And the strengthening food,
The all powerful substance
That kept the Sun alive
Was found
In the human heart.
The Curse of
Tezcatlipoca.

But, even here the Morning Star
Was
The forerunner
Of the Sun.

The tiny Earth spirits watched
The happenings.
They saw

The
Temples of Mitla
Finished
And knew what
They were designed
To do,
And what
They really meant.
They saw the Librarian,
The Great Seer,
Struggle to keep
The memory of the
Lord of the Dawn
Alive
And pure.

At Chichen Itza they saw
The rise
Of
The New Republic
Of the Tree,
Through the image
Of Kukulcan,
The Feathered Serpent,
Watched it fall
Like autumn leaves,
Decay
And return sadly
To Human Sacrifice,
In the
Name of
Quetzalcoatl!

In the Eighth Heaven it began,
And
By the Tenth Heaven
The Mayan Tree
Had grown thorns.

In the Eleventh Heaven
                Some Mayans
                Knew
                What was happening,
                The ones who
                Had stayed in tune
                With creation.

        From D. G. Brinton's
                "The Book of Chilam Balam"
                The words fall
                Like leaves
                Of another autumn,
                Reminiscent of the
                Coming of the
                Lord of the Dawn,
                But this
                came
                nine cycles later.

"Eat, eat, while there is bread,
Drink, drink, while there is water;
A day comes when dust shall darken the air,
When a blight shall wither the land,
When a cloud shall arise,
When a mountain shall be lifted up,
When a strong man shall seize the city.
When ruin shall fall upon all things.
When the tender leaf shall be destroyed
When eyes shall be closed in death,
When there shall be three signs on a tree,
Father, son, and grandson hanging dead on
                the same tree;
When the battle flag shall be raised,
And the people scattered abroad in the Forest."

        And in the Twelfth Heaven
                Among the Aztec came
                This sad song,

A prayer,
A plea
Bitter
With the fruits
Of the
"Tree of Thorns."

"We only came to sleep,
We only came to dream,
It is not true, no, it is not true
That we came to live on the earth.

"We are changed into the grass of springtime;
Our hearts will grow green again
And they will open their petals,
But our body is like a rose tree:
It puts forth flowers and then withers."

The chosen people of the Sun,
            The Aztec.
            Had
            Truly been chosen,
            But
            They knew not
            What task lay before them.
            Nor
            Could they have dreamed
            The scope
            of the tragedy.

The thirteenth Heaven opened with
            A swirl of confusion.
            The entire planet
            seemed to be engulfed
            in some overwhelming restlessness.

The year on the Western Man's calendar
            Was 1467 AD.
            War and rebellion
            raged throughout

the world.
Exploration,
Conquest lay
In the future of Europe.
New frontiers expanding
Across the surface
Of the Earth.

The population of Europe was exploding
At an unbelievable rate of speed,
And
The population wanted
Freedom
And liberty,
And justice.

Drought and epidemics,
Earthquakes
And land slides
Heralded
The coming of the
Prophetic fulfillment
In Mexico.

Drums of restlessness
echoed across
The entire continent.
Time
Had run out.
The Thirteenth Heaven
Was
About to close
And
Moctezuma
Was warned.
First
By his Astrological priesthood,
Then
By

The Earth herself.
More earthquakes,
More devastation,
Popocatepetl
Belched forth a shower of dark smoke
That
Dimmed the sun,
Cinders fell
In the quiet waters
Of Lake Tezcoco.
The hand of death
Was
On the Aztec capitol.
Tenochtitlan
Trembled with fear.
Then
Came
The last evil sign.
It snowed
In the Valley of Mexico,
Turned
The Earth Mother
white.
The people watched
In
Utter astonishment.

Had all this happened before?
Ships--
Ships from the east
And
Ships from the west.
Vikings in Dragon Ships
And
Chinese in Dragon Ships,
Had come from
Different directions.
Some
Had stayed awhile.

Some never left,
Some disappeared.
But
None of them
Changed the ancient prophesy,
The fifty-two year cycles
Continued to count away
The minutes,
Days
And years
Of the
Thirteen Heavens
And the
Nine Hells.
No Viking,
No Chinese
Had changed that pattern,
They, in turn,
Stayed or
Left in astonishment.

The Morning Star had cleared
The horizon of
The Great Eastern Sea.
The place
Was known as
The True Cross,
Veracruz today.
And as the
Morning Star
Rose in the sky
The sun started to show
Its light
Revealing the sails
Of ships.
Ships
With great crosses
Painted on them,
Ships with men

135

In shining metal armour,
Ships
With cannons
And swords
Ships
With horses and saddles,
Great ships
Loaded
With disease.
As the small rowboats
were detached
From the great ships
And started for shore
Their leader asked a question
Of the Catholic Priest
Who sat beside him:
"What is today?"
He asked.
"Good Friday; Senor Cortez,"
The priest answered.
"I know that,
I mean what is the date?"
Cortez said.
"April 21st, 1519,
Senor Cortez,
Have you forgotten?"
"No," said Cortez;
"I didn't forget,
I wondered
If anyone else remembered.
This
Is a Very important day."

"On the Day One Reed
and
The Year One Reed
I shall return.
I will come from
the east
Like the Morning Star"

......Quetzalcoatl

I, Jesus have sent mine angel
to testify unto you these things
in the churches.
I am the root
And the offspring of David,
and
The bright and Morning Star.

......Revelation Chapter 22:16

The Year One Reed
The Day One Reed,
Had come.

LORD OF THE NINE HELLS

Rivers of tears flowed
Through Mexico
Rivers of blood flowed
From
The Heart of the Earth.
Rivers of sorrow,
Rivers of pain,

"Oh, My God, thy water of precious stones
Has fallen
The tall cypress
Has changed into a quetzal bird
The fire serpent
Has been changed into a plumed serpent."

Tenochtitlan had fallen,
Moctezuma was dead,
The Aztec empire fell
Like an aspen leaf
In the mountain breeze
And
Sunk
To the bottom of Lake Tezcoco.

The prophecy of the Lord of the Dawn
Had been completed.
In Oaxaca,
At Mitla,
Not far from
The Tree of Life,
The young Mixtec Priest spoke,
His voice calm,
Assured
That he knew what
Was really happening.

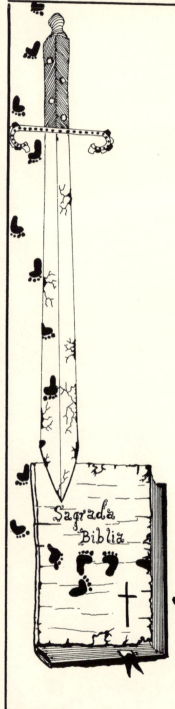

He said, "It has now come to pass,

> We have completed
>
> The Full Cycle,
>
> Our world is done.
>
> As has been before us,
>
> We too shall pass.
>
> The stars
>
> Are falling from the sky,
>
> The water
>
> Is losing its flavor,
>
> Even the rose withers
>
> In this moment of doom.
>
> The earth
>
> Is wrapped with fire,
>
> The sun
>
> Is losing its light,
>
> The moon wanes now
>
> With her final glow.
>
> All is done,
>
> All is over,
>
> Disease and famine stalk our people,
>
> Fear haunts our dreams,
>
> Our world,
>
> Our earth
>
> Is dead."

But the old Librarian,

> The Great Seer,
>
> Said.
>
> "No,
>
> *That is not true*
>
> *That is not what has happened,*

And that
Is not the way it is going to happen.
This
Is the way
It really is, He said.
We have lived
Through thirteen heavens.
Thirteen cycles of fifty-two year epics.
For the first heaven
We were
Pure and simple.
We knew nothing
And
We doubted nothing.
The gifts
Of our Earth Mother
Belonged to all who lived.
The gifts
Were ours
For the taking.
But,
We
Made them complex.
We
Put a value of exchange

To them
And
Each heaven thereafter
Became more restrictive,
We
Became more involved
With
Our own creations
Rather than with
Our Earth Mother
And
Her gifts.
She has not changed,
She
Is the same beautiful sphere
That
She was in the beginning
Her gifts
Still spring from her flesh,
She
Still gives all to her children.
We
Have changed.
Perhaps not all of us have changed,
Perhaps not all of us have forgotten.

We have ended the Thirteen Heavens,
We will now
Enter
The Nine Hells,
Now
Things will change.

Foreign lords with foreign gods
Have come
With greater power.
They,
Understand nothing about us,

Nor
Do they really desire
To
Know our stories,
Our histories.
They
Will impose
Their way
Upon us
And
We will hear them,
And
Believe them
Or
We will die.
Many of us will die anyway,
It matters little
What we believe.
We
Will grow our crops
For them,
Toil in the field
For them.
Sweat in the shops
For them.
We
Will forsake our Gods,
For them.
Their holy men,
Their sacred books,
Their prophecies
Shall prevail.
Ours
Will be thought the prattle of children,
Our temples
Will give way
To theirs,
Our altars
Will be replaced

By theirs,
Our holy places
Will   become
Places of mystery
To them.
They,
These foreigners
Know even less about
The Earth Mother
Than
We do,
And
They care
Even less.

But the Creator has a Master plan,
And
What these foreigners
Don't know,
Or
What they have forgotten
Will be remembered
Before
The end of the Ninth Hell.
You see,
Their prophecies
Are also
Our prophecies,
Their sacred books
Are also
Our sacred books,
And ours
Belong to them as well.

The great-grandchildren of these foreigners
Will dig
In the dust,
Hunting for clues

To
What we are,
What is now
Being destroyed.

Prepare yourself for death
My
Young men and women
Of the Order of the
Lord of The Dawn,
Because
The Lord of the Nine Hells
Has come,
His name is Tezcatlipoca."

The population of Mexico
Between the Isthmus of Tehuantepec
And the
Valley of Mexico
Is estimated at between
Twenty and twenty-eight million
People
At the time of the conquest.
One Hell later,
Fifty-two years
From the time
Cortez landed at Veracruz
The population
Of that part of Mexico
Was
Reduced
To less than one million people.

The end did not come
With the Spanish Conquest
For the Spaniard,
Like the Pilgrim Fathers,
And the founders of Jamestown,
Was

In truth
Only executor
Of a prophecy
Laid down
Long ago and
The inner secrets
Of that prophecy
were not only known
In Ancient Mexico,
Nor even restricted to the Americas,
People,
Holy men,
Keepers of the books,
Disciples of the various Manifestations
All over the world
Knew
Parts of This prophecy,
And,
To the best of their ability
They prepared
To meet
The challenge.

Tezcatlipoca was his name
In Mexico,
But
He is known throughout
The world.
He has always been
The god of warriors,
The god of thieves,
The god of bigots,
The god of blood sacrifice,
The god of horror
and
The god of gossip.
It is he
Who stills
The souls

146

Of those
Who follow him.

The philosophy of Tezcatlipoca
Is exemplified
In this quotation
From
Alfonso Casos'
Aztecs; People of the Sun.

"Since he was young, he was the first to arrive
at the festivities when the gods returned, in
the month of Teotleco. He carried off old
Tlaloc's wife, Xochiquetzal, goddess of flowers
and love, of whom he said:

"I believe that she is truly a goddess,
That she is really very beautiful and fine.
I shall have her, not tomorrow, nor the
next day, nor the next, but right now, at
this moment, for I, in person, am he who
ordains and commands it so. I am the
Young Warrior who shines like the sun and has
The beauty of the dawn."

* From *The Aztecs: People of
the Sun,* by Alfonso Caso.
© 1958 by the University of
Oklahoma Press.

The philosophy of Tezcatlipoca
Is direct and
Without flowery phrases.
Rape,
Murder,
Steal,
Lie,
Control,
Torture,
He with the greater club
Is right,
He with no club
Toils.

And those holy men,

The keepers-of-the-book

Knew

That on April 21, 1519 AD

It

Was not

The coming of Tezcatlipoca,

It

Was in truth

The day he started to work.

He is a great master,

He wears a strange mask

And before

The end of the Ninth Hell

He will

Take it off

And all of us

Will be surprised

Who

He

Really is.

"THE REQUIEM"

The Mass celebrated for the repose of
the souls of the dead. . . .

Webster's Dictionary

THE REQUIEM

The Little People, the Tlaloques and Pockwatchies
Watched on.
They saw
The dark shadow fall
Across the lands.
Saw the battles fought,
The drums silenced,
Saw
The Father,
Son,
And Grandson
Hang from the same tree.
Watched the railways
Span the plains,
Saw the buffalo disappear,
The tribes
Herded like cattle
Onto reservations.
Heard the newborn babies cry
And
Saw them buried

In lonely frozen graves
Far
From their original homes
Heard
The death song
Of
Crazy Horse.
Saw
Sitting Bull
murdered,
The Ghost Dance
Rise and fall
And
Father Peyote
Attempt a return,
And fail.

And they were the witness to
The Rivers of filth,
Destruction of forests,
Devastation of land,
Pollution of lakes,
They saw
The springs disappear,
Like hidden tears.
And
They mourned
The
Untimely decay
Of
Their Earth Mother.
They saw
The tender leaf destroyed
And
The mountain lifted up,
The canyons filled in.
They saw
The cities rise

And
Watched
The smoke settle
And
Heard
The groan
Of a people in despair.

The Little People knew
What was happening,
But
They could not stop it,
And
They knew that.

The atom bomb is by all means
The
Greatest destroying force
Ever used by man
Against
Man.

It is the energy of the
Sun
Trapped
On earth.

When the first test was made
At
White Sands, New Mexico
July 16, 1945,
The scientists
Gasped
At the power
They
Now held in their hands.

According to the prophecy
We

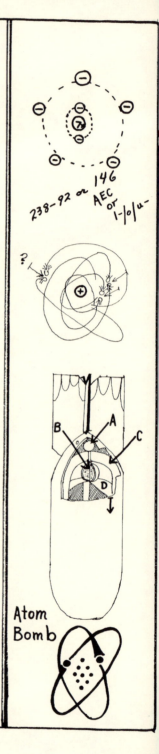

Atom
Bomb

Entered the ninth hell
On
August 3, 1935.
In
March of that year
Adolph Hitler
Startled the world
When
He denounced the clauses
Of the
Versailles Treaty
Providing for
German disarmament.

The swastica, with its chosen superman philosophy,
Had
Started to rise.
And,
As with the Aztecs before them,
The Germans
Used the slogan
"We are the Super-race,
The chosen people,
Set forth to justify
The wrongs of man,
We are all wise,
All sound,
All intelligent,
We
Will rule,
Today Berlin,
Tomorrow the world."

"Today Tenochtitlan, tomorrow the world

        And our god

        Is the

        Sun,"

        Said the Aztec.

Ten years and three days

        After

        We entered

        The Ninth Hell,

        On August 6, 1945,

        The first

        Atom bomb was dropped

        On

        Hiroshima, Japan.

        The world

        was stunned

        When

        Three days later

        On

        August 9, 1945,

        The second bomb

        Struck

        Nagasaki.

        The

        Power of the Sun-god

        On Earth!

It is interesting to note that

        The atom bomb

        was assembled

        At

        Los Alamos, New Mexico.

        Los Alamos is

        The

        Spanish name

        For

        Cottonwood Tree.

The war is over! some said.

But,

Is it

Really over.

Was the

Second World War

In truth

The opening of the Ninth Hell.

The world

Has

Not felt rest,

Realized peace

Since that horrible date ?

In August of 1935.

Mounting tensions,

Religious decay,

Mass confusion,

War,

Strife,

And intrigue

Has brought

All people

To

An awareness

That

Something is happening,

Something

We cannot control.

Racial identity, Youth identity,
Racial and youth rebellion,
Followed by
An international explosion
Of
Drug addiction
Moral and political decay,
Rape,
Murder,
Robbery
Are common words among
Our third grade Americans.

The Philosophy of
Tezcatlipoca.

Is God dead?
What is happening
To our children?
Will
This Hell
Ever end?

Yes!
It will end on
August 16, 1987.

What will happen then?
Will all of this
Be
destroyed,
Will the earth
Be
Blown up
And
All of this be
Lost,
What   will happen?

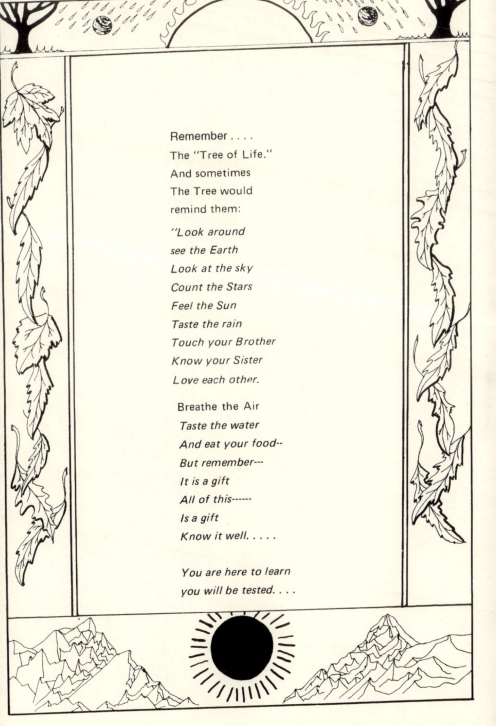

Remember . . . .
The "Tree of Life."
And sometimes
The Tree would
remind them:

"Look around
see the Earth
Look at the sky
Count the Stars
Feel the Sun
Taste the rain
Touch your Brother
Know your Sister
Love each other.

Breathe the Air
Taste the water
And eat your food--
But remember---
It is a gift
All of this------
Is a gift
Know it well. . . . .

You are here to learn
you will be tested. . . .

An old, white haired Zapotec farmer
Stood
At the roots
Of the Tree.
He
Was looking upward
At a
Bright glowing spot
On
The trunk.

Thunder rolled through the sky,
Distant at first,
Lightning
Bounced
From cloud to cloud.
The heavens grew dark
With heavy rain
Now
Moving more rapidly
Toward the Tree,
Thunder boomed,
Lightning exploded,
Lighting
The Valley of Oaxaca
With
A
Bright blue light.

The Zapotec moved not a muscle
Of his body.
His jaw was set,
His eyes reflecting
The astonishment
He felt.

From the bright spot on
The Tree trunk
Pockwatchies
were coming.
First one,
Then more,
A dozen of the little people
coming fast,
Followed by
Even more,
Singing as they came.
They wore stars on their wrists
And
Carried God Eyes in their hands.
Dancing in flight,
They passed by the old man
And
He could hear their brave song,
Never heard before,
Not even
By them.

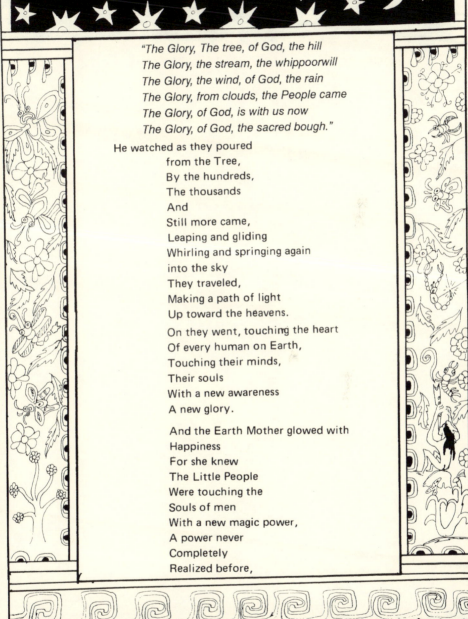

"The Glory, The tree, of God, the hill
The Glory, the stream, the whippoorwill
The Glory, the wind, of God, the rain
The Glory, from clouds, the People came
The Glory, of God, is with us now
The Glory, of God, the sacred bough."

He watched as they poured
     from the Tree,
     By the hundreds,
     The thousands
     And
     Still more came,
     Leaping and gliding
     Whirling and springing again
     into the sky
     They traveled,
     Making a path of light
     Up toward the heavens.

     On they went, touching the heart
     Of every human on Earth,
     Touching their minds,
     Their souls
     With a new awareness
     A new glory.

     And the Earth Mother glowed with
     Happiness
     For she knew
     The Little People
     Were touching the
     Souls of men
     With a new magic power,
     A power never
     Completely
     Realized before,

A power
That awakened responsibility
In
Every soul,
A
Responsibility
To the Earth Mother.
For
Now
Mankind
Had been made
The Guardian
Of
The
Earth Mother.
And man would be given greater powers
Than
He had ever dreamed.
He
Had been tested
And
He had succeeded.
He
Would now truly
Be
A
Part of the Universe.
And the tiny Earth Spirits
Disappeared
And
Were never seen again,
For
They now lived
In
The hearts of men.

162

"It is true!" said the Zapotec,
"Yes,
It is true,"
He stepped closer to
The huge Tree,
Much closer.

"The Glory of God is with us now
The Glory of God, the sacred bough . . ."
And
The Clouds
Drenched
The Earth
With
Love. . . . .

Tonatiuh's face (the face of the sun) who was the Lord of Heaven, around which took place all daily or periodic phenomena. The crown, nose, pendant, earrings, and necklace are most luxurious and are the ornaments proper of this deity. The hair was fair due to the golden appearance of the star; the wrinkles on the face were to show great maturity or age; and the tongue, like an obsidian knife stuck outward

Ehecatonatiuh (Sun of Wind), "Second Epoch, at the end of which humanity was destroyed by strong winds. The gods transformed human beings into apes in order that they might cling better and not be carried away by the hurricanes, thus originating the similarity between the human race and the Simians..." This was because large forests had been found razed by tornadoes.

Plate of the consecration and dedication of this stone with the date 13 – acatl, (13 – Reed) Equivalent to the year of 1479 A.D.

Ocelotonatiuh (Sun of Jaguar), was the "first and most remote of the four cosmogonic epochs, in which the giants, who had been created by the gods, lived. They did not till the soil and lived in caves, ate wild fruits and roots, and were finally attacked and devoured by the jaguars..." The basic epoch of the Aztecs goes back to the quaternary, since they discovered bones of pre-diluvian animals buried in deep gullies below dense lithospheric layers.

Quiauhtonatiuh (Sun of Fire - Rain), "Third cosmogonic epoch, in which everything was extinguished by the rain of lava and fire. Men were transformed at this time into birds, thus saving themselves from the slaughter..." They justified this belief due to the many signs of volcanic activities in our territory and also on account of the discovery of huts and skeletons under layers of lava and ashes.

Nahui - Ollin (Sun of Earthquake). Fifth epoch in their solar age; it means the next and last destruction of human life in the world. This symbol is used here as a frame for the central signs.

Atonatiuh (Sun of Water), "means the fourth epoch, at the end of which everything perished because of terrific storms and torrential rains that covered the earth, reaching the peaks of the highest mountains. The gods changed men into fishes to save them from this universal deluge..." The discovery of different fossilized species of marine fauna on the top of the mountains created the basis for this belief.

← The Eagle Bowl with the 20 day signs and the Ollin symbol highlighted.

The Ollin symbol from the 20 Day

AFTERWORD
Looking Back to 1964

I asked my publisher if I might have a few pages to share these final thoughts. I am now a man in my late sixties, and for the past thirty years my entire existence has revolved around this book. If you examine the conditions that existed on Native American reservations before 1964 and if you consider the conditions of life for all Mexican and Central American Indians at that same time, when thousands of Mayan people in Guatamala—men, women and children—were slaughtered like pests; then you will have a notion of what ignited and drove me into action to try to change all of that, what finally led me to write this book, and what later caused me to take it to the world. I believe that God gave me a choice in how to spend my temporary earthly existence. I regard myself as a true poet, a man who does not desire much in the monetary scene. My poetic urge led me to Ce Acatl Quetzalcoatl, and it was Quetzalcoatl that I selected as my champion to fight for the rights of Indian people in Mexico and Central America.

I remember my position in those days. From the fountainhead of network television, I watched the corruption of our government. War in Vietnam. Assassinations. Watergate. Nixon. Johnson and all the rest of it. I had a ringside seat to it all. I had become *the man with the gray flannel head*. My life belonged to an electronic monster that stood for everything that I disliked about a country I love—America. My boss was TV, and TV could not make a stand for the earth that was being raped by stupidity and greed, for Native American or Chicano rights, for the murders that were happening to whole villages of Mayan people in Central America. My boss was a hungry giant that was as helpless as an inchworm in an anthill. I worked with all of that, and I wanted to change it if I could. At heart I was a poet who had fallen in love with a valley and a people. More than that, I had found a tree, and met an Indian woman, the girl of my dreams, who helped me come to know the importance of the tree. So I quit TV, went to live in the Valley of Oaxaca, and there, infused with inspiration and the collection of much valuable information, the words to *LORD OF THE DAWN* began to spring forth.

But it was not meant to last. What I had learned in Oaxaca had become a story that I desired to give to the world. For me, I had found the meaning of God in a valley, in a people and in the inspiration of an old tree. And in the love of a simple and plain Indian woman who had given depth to my life. Alicia loved the tree equally as much as I, and for the same reasons. Our life was good together. We loved each other and loved the world we lived in. Through her I learned many values of real Indian people. I learned the importance of respect for the rights of others, which is the foundation of peace and harmony. She told me that Christ is not dead, but that he had been transformed, he was alive. At first I didn't understand, but I began to think about the Christ story and the Quetzalcoatl story. I began to see similarities. I thought about the story of White Buffalo Calf Woman of the Lakota and Sky Woman of the Iroquois. I began to think about all of the similar stories in human history from the world of Europeans and Asians. They are one story with one promise. We know it from oppressed people everywhere. It is the promise of a time when justice will come to dwell in the world, when a sacred man or a sacred woman will come to teach us the ways of peace and harmony. Ce Acatl Quetzalcoatl was such a sacred man. He taught respect and care for all living things, and showed us how that respect can blossom into a new reality. I experienced that reality and respect, in a small way, in Oaxaca during those golden days of inspiration.

But Oaxaca was not my home, the Zapotec were not my people, and time had run out for Alicia and me. And so it ended where it had began; it ended at the roots of the great tree. It ended with us lighting two candles at the altar of Guadalupe, the Virgin Mother of Indian people, with our thanking God that we had met. It ended with us knowing that the love we had found in each other would always be there. From all of that love and joy, pain and sorrow, this story of a sacred Mexican Indian was put to paper. It included a prophecy of a new world coming, of a new nobler race to walk upon the earth, a prophecy that promised justice for all people. I believe that that justice is called The Glory of God.

BACKGROUND HISTORY

THE SACRED CALENDAR, AN ALMANAC

Above is pictured my old flute, three of my favorite books, and a replica of the so called Aztec Calendar Stone. Also pictured is a candle, which symbolizes time. The last section of this book is about time. And I think it is about time that we stop calling that replica the Aztec Calendar, because it is not the calendar, but rather the Eagle Bowl or "Sun Stone." It represents the cosmology of the Tenochca, who were the citizens of Tenochititlan, now Mexico City, the largest city in the world. The Tenochca have come to be called the Aztec. Through misinformation people still call the Eagle Bowl the Aztec Calendar.

Actually the real calendar is a mathematical field of 260 days, 260 combinations of "day signs" (hieroglyphics) and magical numbers. This is accomplished by a multiplication of the 13 numbers times the 20 day signs. 13 x 20 = 260. This formula of 13 x 20 is an amazing time keeping tool which was virtually unknown to the rest of the ancient world. It is the most characteristic time count of Mesoamerica. It was called Tonalpohulli (Count of Days) by the Tenochca, Tzolkin (Wheel of Days) by the Maya, and Pije by the Zapotec. It was known to every nation of Mesoamerican people, and we can be sure that the formula, in an altered form, was used by people far away from its Mexican homeland. After years of investigation, it is my opinion that the sacred calendar was derived from the mystery of the human female body, and that the 260 days approximate the birthing cycle, from conception to the delivery of a human child. It was certainly used by the Tenochca to create the twenty-five ton monolith we call the Eagle Bowl. Using the 260 day calendar, one can plot the movements of the cosmos, balance the solar year, predict returning comets, and measure the cycles of time. It also worked like a Farmers' Almanac, indicating days for planting and days of harvest. Because of its relationship with the seed, it could also be used as a device to plan parenthood. The ancients must have understood that if used this way, 260 days after conception a child would be born. Let's say that the parents desired a child born on or around the first day of the calendar, which is "1 Alligator." In 260 days after conception the child would be born, on the same day, or close to the same day, of the calendar that it was conceived, "1 Alligator." The child would be given its family name, but also given the name of the day of the calendar on which it was born, "1 Alligator." Of course, there were no guarantees.

On the next page are a few exercises to get started. You can copy and enlarge the diagram below for easy reference. My Zapotec teachers took me

1. Cipactli (Alligator)	1	8	2	9	3	10	4	11	5	12	6	13	7
2. Ehecatl (Wind)	2	9	3	10	4	11	5	12	6	13	7	1	8
3. Calli (House)	3	10	4	11	5	12	6	13	7	1	8	2	9
4. Cuetzpallin (Lizard)	4	11	5	12	6	13	7	1	8	2	9	3	10
5. Coatl (Serpent)	5	12	6	13	7	1	8	2	9	3	10	4	11
6. Miquiztli (Death)	6	13	7	1	8	2	9	3	10	4	11	5	12
7. Mazatl (Deer)	7	1	8	2	9	3	10	4	11	5	12	6	13
8. Tochtl (Rabbit)	8	2	9	3	10	4	11	5	12	6	13	7	1
9. Atl (Water)	9	3	10	4	11	5	12	6	13	7	1	8	2
10. Itzcuintli (Dog)	10	4	11	5	12	6	13	7	1	8	2	9	3
11. Ozomatli (Monkey)	11	5	12	6	13	7	1	8	2	9	3	10	4
12. Malinalli (Grass)	12	6	13	7	1	8	2	9	3	10	4	11	5
13. Acatl (Reed)	13	7	1	8	2	9	3	10	4	11	5	12	6
14. Ocelotl (Jaguar)	1	8	2	9	3	10	4	11	5	12	6	13	7
15. Cuauhtli (Eagle)	2	9	3	10	4	11	5	12	6	13	7	1	8
16. Cozcacuauhtli (Buzzard)	3	10	4	11	5	12	6	13	7	1	8	2	9
17. Ollin (Earthquake)	4	11	5	12	6	13	7	1	8	2	9	3	10
18. Tecpatl (Flint Knife)	5	12	6	13	7	1	8	2	9	3	10	4	11
19. Quiahuitl (Rain)	6	13	7	1	8	2	9	3	10	4	11	5	12
20. Xochitl (Flower)	7	1	8	2	9	3	10	4	11	5	12	6	13

The Sacred Calendar of 260 days. NOTE: The bold lines have only been added to this diagram of the calendar to distinguish its four quarters and the ease of use for readers.

into areas of the calendar that became a source of "amazed joy" for me. The more information I learned, the more fun I had exploring various possibilities. Eventually, I used my findings to create the prophecy and to write this book about my findings.

Seventy-three of these 260-day calendar years equals 52 solar years of 365 days. (Try it on your calculator.) This 52 year cycle was regarded the same as we regard a century. The Indians "collected" the ¼ days that we use in a leap year for 52 years and added 13 days to the end of each 52 year cycle. There is more—all very amazing, all very dependable, and all very ancient.

1. Every number is always surrounded by the same collection of numbers.

2. If you subtract the first number from the next number to its right, you will always get 7.

3. Reverse the process and you will always get 6.

4. (For this example I have divided the calendar into four quarters. Since there are 13 horizontal columns I have outlined the middle column. We will come back to that 7th column later.) Start with the corner numbers, upper left 1, upper right 7, lower left 7, lower right 13. Now add them up to get 28.

5. Next, balance any number against its counterpart in the same way and you will always get 28. (But what about that middle column? How can we balance it against the other numbers?)

```
*
**
***
****
*****
******
*******
=28
```

6. With the middle column, we balance it against itself. The top two numbers are added to the bottom two numbers to get 28. Then the next pair, and so forth—always 28.

7. The next and last exercise is the counting process. It goes like this. How many kernels of corn does it take to count to 7 using vertical column number 1? Each dot represents a kernel of corn.

Following this process through each of the vertical columns will create different geometric patterns, which, when laid side by side and placed together in various ways, become works of art. Remember, there are 13 vertical columns and 20 horizontal columns to work with. If you enjoy puzzles, you are in for a great treat, plus a little diversion from the Five O'Clock Evening News.

I suspect that the calendar was used as much for entertainment as it was for magical and scientific purposes. If you explore into it, using your imagination, you will make discoveries of your own. We have television, they had the calendar. We have the computer, and so did they. It is not difficult to see in this ancient tool a forerunner to our modern electronic Apple or IBM machines. It is as if this incredible time counter is a "chip" from a much larger device. As we allow our creative imaginations to play within the limitations of the calendar we will discover new possibilities. At first we recognize the 28 days as the Moon cycle of the human female. Later, we see it as the 28 year cycle of the planet Saturn. We look backward or forward at our own Saturn cycle, and perhaps we ask, "How many Saturn cycles are there in a lifetime?"

From the calendar we become aware of our relationship with the planets of the cosmos. Mars with 780 synodical days in its year—3 x 260 = 780. As we use the numbers, we gain respect for the astronomers of Monte Alban, Tajin, Zampoala, Chichen Itza, Uxmal, Kabah, and the beautiful Palenque. In all of these ancient cities we find the calendar still at work. At Mitla, in Oaxaca, we can best grasp its great works of art through the visions created by the calendar. Without the visions created by the calendar we will never really understand these ancient cities at all. The calendar is a bridge between two totally different realities, that of the non-Indian who came and unfortunately destroyed so much of beauty, so much of the sacred, and that of the native people, who had learned many secrets from the gift of the sacred calendar. But in the end they had no way to protect themselves. The calendar taught them that one day the Gift Bringer would return. It also taught them that all things must be in balance, and that that takes time and practice. If there is one thing that I have learned from the calendar, it is this. The Great Mystery is still the Great Mystery.

THE EAGLE BOWL

In my book Beneath the Moon and Under the Sun, I offered my readers a more comprehensive understanding of the Eagle Bowl. In the next few paragraphs I will explain the idea of the five past worlds carved on the Eagle Bowl, vent my feelings in regard to the future of the Sixth World, and touch upon a few interesting highlights along the way.

In 1479, just thirteen years before Christopher Columbus discovered America, the mighty emperor of Tenochtitlan dedicated a work of art that would one day become the most celebrated piece of Native American art in existence. On a twenty-five ton hunk of basalt the artists of the Tenochca carved a circle which measures about twelve feet in diameter. Within the circumference of the circle they carved, in symbols and glyphs, one of the most extraordinary cosmologies ever conceived by humankind, using the sacred calendar as its rule, and the ancient myths as its theme. Volumes have been written about this amazing mandala and the proud people who loved and understood its unique concept of life and death. Many of those values are found within the pages of this book. Most of them are still held by the people of modern Mexico. To know the story of the Eagle Bowl is to know the history of Mexico.

Looking at the Eagle Bowl on page 164, we see that the First World is called "Sun of Jaguar," followed to the left by "Sun of Wind," next, lower left, "Sun of Fire Rain," and to the lower right "Sun of Water." I have darkened the borders of the symbol for the Fifth Sun, which is called, "Sun of Earthquake," or as I prefer it, "Sun of Movement." The Ollin symbol, which means both "movement" and "earthquake," dominates the center of the Eagle Bowl and embraces the four past worlds. Each of these worlds, according to tradition, was destroyed when the next world was created. The Tenochca, and other people of Mexico, believed that in the future the Fifth World would also be destroyed and a new world would be born. But no one knew when or if that

Twenty day signs as they appear on the Eagle Bowl

would really happen. Nonetheless, the fear of doom weakened the will of the people and made them easy targets for the conquering Spaniards. They feared that the sun would die, and the world would be plunged into darkness. In order to keep the sun strong and healthy, the Tenochca started holy wars, seeking victims whose hearts could be fed to the sun. They seriously believed that this would save the world and make the gods happy. They had forgotten the fact that this sun was symbolic, and not real. They had become like the curator who became lost in his own museum.

My claim is that on August 16, 1987 the Fifth Sun symbolically died and we entered the Sixth Sun, the Sixth World. My reasoning for this claim is based on a calendar formula derived from a Mayan belief in Thirteen Heavens and Nine Hells. The time cycle of each of the past worlds is measurable by these heavens and hells. Each heaven and each hell is represented by a 52 year cycle (already mentioned). Thirteen heavens plus nine hells equals twenty-two. 22 x 52 = 1144 years, which is the measurement of any one world. Then five worlds times 1144 years = 5720. This is an interesting number of years because the Jewish calendar, measuring the time from Eden, counts 5747 years in 1987. Two calendars, one from Mexico, the other from Israel, and with only 27 years of difference in this very long period of time!

A more detailed study corroborates these claims. For example, Covarrubias tells us that "The Maya attributed a fabulous antiquity to their history. They counted time from a zero date, the mythical beginning of the world, '4 ahua, 8 cumhu,' which Spinden interprets as 'October 15, 3375 B.C.', some five thousand years ago, a time that coincides curiously with the calculated beginning of civilization in the Old World."

More recent information claims that the dates mentioned above are incorrect, as much as 260 years off. Still other correlations disagree with that, and so forth. Whatever the case may be, the calendar was created as a means to join people together in a common understanding of time, not as a means to cause further chaos and prejudice. We do not need an ancient calendar to recognize the chaos brought on by the lack of balance in the world today. On the one hand, we see the breakdown of everything that would bring the world to peace and harmony. On the other hand, we find a world that is bursting with willingness to re-establish loyalty and compassion, amenable to clean up the mess we have all contributed to.

In the seven years that have passed since August 16, 1987 our world has stumbled through some of the most remarkable changes ever imagined. These changes have been both good and not so good. And there are even more changes before us. Some people have given up, believing that there are no answers to such frightening problems. Others have turned their backs and pretended that "all is well." I am still of the opinion that a new world, the Sixth World, has been born, and that this new world is like an infant born amidst violent surroundings, needing care and nurturing so that it can survive. It needs both physical and spiritual support. We must love it for what it really is, which is a part of God's work.

THE LITTLE PEOPLE

Constructing an epic work from poetic myth is as difficult as writing a factual story from historic events. There is a responsibility involved in both approaches to the story. The responsibility is to the reader of the work. The author must make it clear what path they are taking. In this book, it is clear that the author is deeply involved in a poetic myth that is more often derived from the tradition of a certain valley and people, from a great tree, or from the haunting memories of a woman that he loved, than it is derived from the pages of scholarly works of ethnology. I take the stories told to me by a Zapotec shepherd or Mexico City cab driver as serious sources of information. Nonetheless the work is not merely "wanton figments" of my imagination but is logically deduced from reputable ethnic traditions and documents.

Much of its success depends on the proper understanding of the "little people" who play an important role in the delivery of Quetzalcoatl's message to the modern world. To the ancient people of southern Mexico, they were believed to be the servants of the rain god, Tlaloc (Casijo in Oaxaca). The creator appointed them to be guardians of the Earth Mother at the beginning of the First Creation. In the minds of the ancient Americans, they not only existed on this earth but in the Rain Paradise of another world. The size of these little folk seems to depend on who is telling the story and why they are telling it. Many believed them to be less than three inches tall but extremely powerful, for they could bring rain, cause lightning and thunder, and influence people. Whether they actually exist or not is unimportant compared to their symbolic significance, for they signify whatever preserves beauty and harmony in our living world. Their spiritual death in our hearts, that is our inability to be sensitive to our beautiful creation and its preservation, means the material destruction of our planet through human greed and blindness; for where there are no pockwatchies to be found, you will see pollution, violence, cruelty, discord, and so forth. Where there are no pockwatchies ego has destroyed bliss, and lust has destroyed love. Where you find love, you will find pockwatchie power at work.

The names for the "little people" are many and known to nearly all the tribes of Indian people. In *The Popol Vuh: Sacred Book of the Quiche Maya*, by Goetz and Morley, we read of them. Here they are called "the guardians of the woods, the spirits of the mountains." *U vinaquil* is literally "the little man of the forest." They are similar to the *alux* of the modern Maya. The Cakchiquel call them *ru vinakil chee* from "tree," translated as "spirits which walk in the mountains." In ancient times the Cakchiquel could speak with these little people who were the spirits of the volcano Fuego. The Mazatecs still believe in such little people, some of whom can cause illness, like the *la-a*. The *chikushi* provide rain if properly called upon. The Zoques tell stories of ancient little men with baby faces called *mo-yo*, who hide treasures and store the best corn in caves. They carry serpents that are really thunderbolts. The Popolucas of Vera Cruz have *chanis*, "masters of game and fish," and *hunchuts*, who live behind waterfalls, fall in love with beautiful women, and sometimes even kidnap and marry them. The Zapotecs have their *bize* and *bizi-a*, who live in caves and carry lightning in their hands. These are the same as the *tlaloques*, servants of the rain god, Tlaloc. Henry Wadsworth Longfellow wrote about the little people in *Hiawatha*. He called them *pau-puk-keewis*. I suspect that that is the source of the name *pockwatchie* that I use often in my stories. It could be that a *pau-puk-keewi* married a *bize* from Oaxaca, and they called their offspring *pockwatchies*! Next time I talk to Quill, I'll ask him about it. But knowing Quill as I do, he will only laugh and say something like, "It doesn't matter what you call us."

Children standing around part of the trunk of the "Tree" at Oaxaca in Mexico.

THE TREE OF THE WORLD

Imagine how the world was 4,000 years ago. The Valley of Oaxaca was a shallow lake or a deep swamp then. A forest of cypress trees grew along the shore line. Dark woods covered the steep slopes of Monte Alban. Families of humans lived together there for protection against the elements. No one alive then would have believed the eminent history that would one day be written about this place. The valley was still an untamed wilderness.

But on a tiny island somewhere in that dreary swamp a miracle was beginning to take place. The warmth of the sun had awakened the life force in a little seed that was hidden just below the surface of the earth. The seed cracked and opened, sending a tiny root downward, sending a tiny stem upward. The breast of the earth opened and the tiny stem appeared for all the world to see. The biggest tree in the world had just been born. The Creator, the Balancer, the All Knowing, the All Wise, smiled and said, "Good."

The great tree of Oaxaca holds its awesome position as one of the noblest living plants on earth. It measures 150 feet in circumference, 36 feet in diameter, 114 feet in height. By species it is a Montezuma Bald Cypress. You may visit this masterpiece in the village churchyard of Santa Maria del Tule a few miles east of Oaxaca. Based upon the thickness of the tree it has been estimated to be 6,000 years old. Recently it was decided that it is not one tree, but three trees grown together. Tree experts are in disagreement as to its exact age, but it is safe to assume that it is no less than 4,000 years old, and perhaps far older.

Legend has it that Hernando Cortez visited the tree in 1520. I doubt that for practical reasons. But I do not doubt that an Indian temple once stood where the Catholic cathedral now stands. The name of the village suggests that the old temple was dedicated to a goddess, perhaps Quetzalcoatl's mother, Chimalma Tonantzin. It was customary in the days of the conquest to destroy an Indian temple, then rename the place with a Christian equivalent. In translation the name of the village is Saint Mary of the Swamp, Mary being the mother of Jesus, Tonantzin being the ancient Mother of all the gods. The Indians had no trouble accepting this difference. But the dark robed Catholic priests were troubled with the idea, and they still are. They cannot understand that the Sacred Woman belongs to all people and all faiths.

As recently as 1921 a freshwater spring flowed from the roots of the tree. But the spring dried up and disappeared as the water table of the valley lowered. Now there is not a sign of the spring. Once the spring was gone the church constructed an iron fence around the colossal tree in hopes of protecting the giant from intruders. They placed a sign there stating that the tree was 2,000 years old, which is not at all true. I guess they wanted the great tree and Jesus to have something in common.

When a tree has lived as many years as this primeval giant, you can be sure that there are as many stories about the tree as it has branches. One of these stories is about a phantom lady that dwells within the tree. This ghostly woman brings no harm. She is a friend to children and women who have been abused. Some stories tell that she has been seen far away from the tree, particularly along the Pan-American highway between Tule and Tehuantepec. There she has saved the lives of many travelers on the dangerous mountain road. On several occasions she has wakened a drowsing bus driver moments before he would have crashed off the highway. Who is this woman? The answer is always the same, "She will always be a mystery—one of the many mysteries kept secret by the tree."